Dog eat Doug

It's a Good Thing They're Cute

by Brian Anderson

Andrews McMeel
Publishing, LLC

Kansas City

08 09 10 11 12 TWP 10 9 8 7 6 5 4 3 2 1

ISBN-13: 978-0-7407-7366-2
ISBN-10: 0-7407-7366-6

Library of Congress Control Number: 2008921599

www.andrewsmcmeel.com

─── **ATTENTION: SCHOOLS AND BUSINESSES** ───

Andrews McMeel books are available at quantity discounts with bulk purchase for educational, business, or sales promotional use. For information, please write to: Special Sales Department, Andrews McMeel Publishing, LLC, 1130 Walnut Street, Kansas City, Missouri 64106.

For Mom and Dad

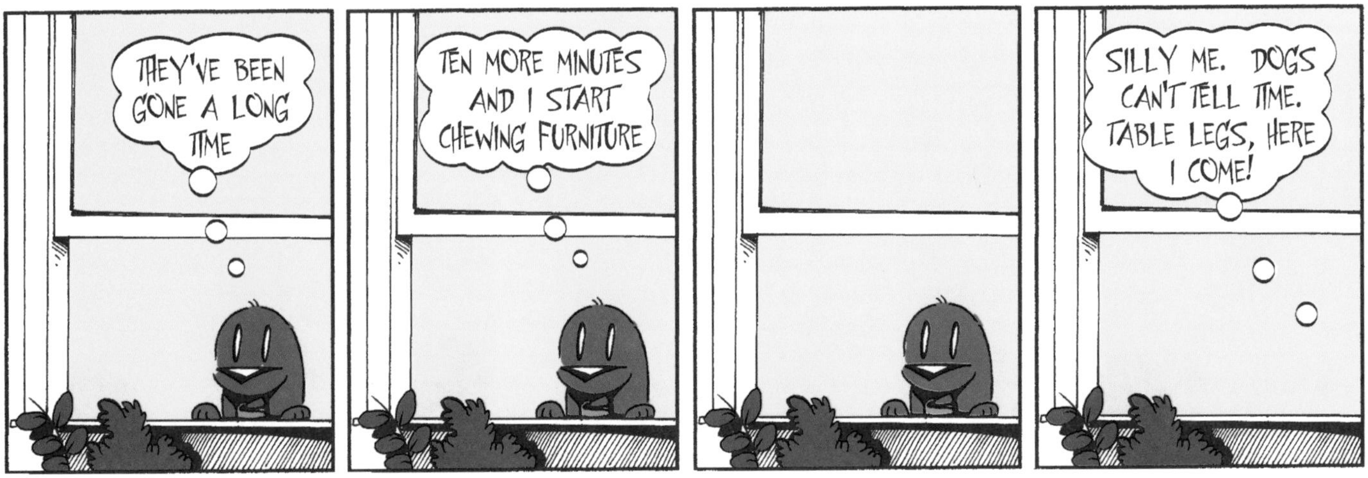
THEY'VE BEEN GONE A LONG TIME
TEN MORE MINUTES AND I START CHEWING FURNITURE
SILLY ME. DOGS CAN'T TELL TIME. TABLE LEGS, HERE I COME!

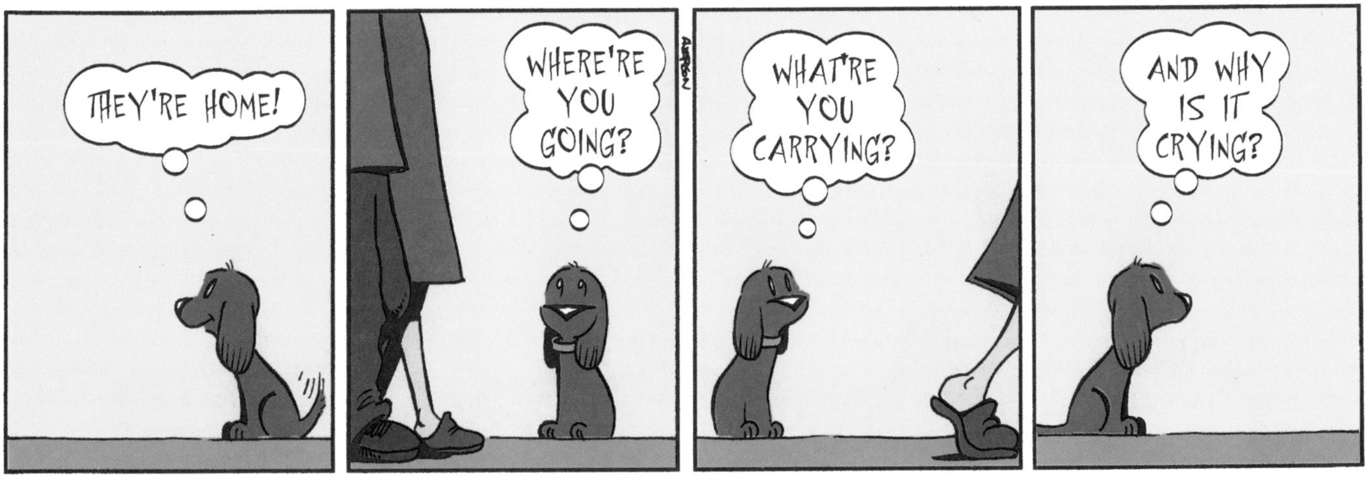
THEY'RE HOME!
WHERE'RE YOU GOING?
WHAT'RE YOU CARRYING?
AND WHY IS IT CRYING?

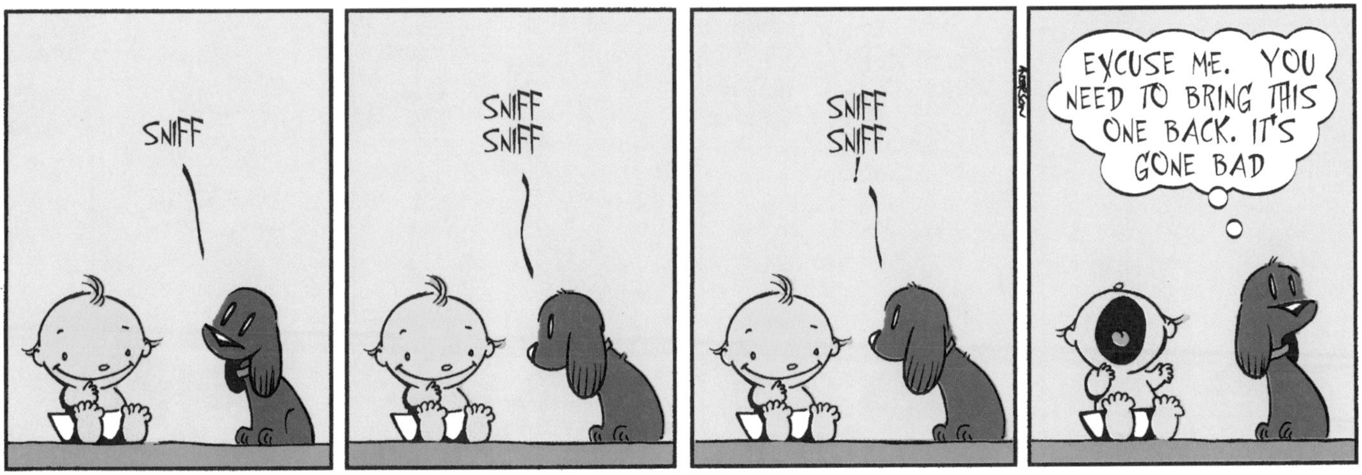
SNIFF
SNIFF SNIFF
SNIFF SNIFF !
EXCUSE ME. YOU NEED TO BRING THIS ONE BACK. IT'S GONE BAD

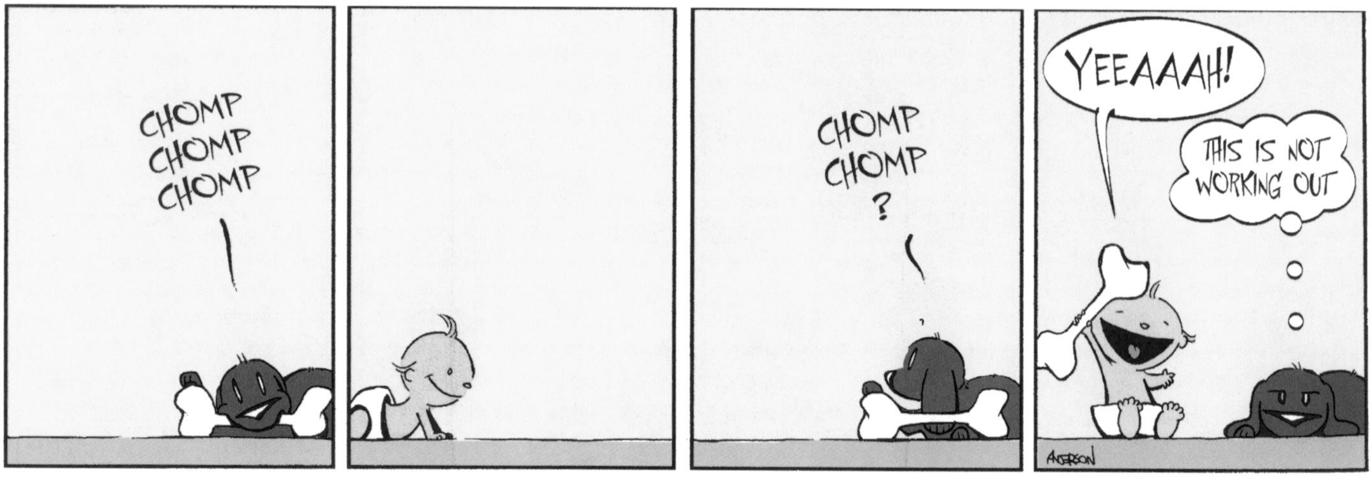
CHOMP CHOMP CHOMP
CHOMP CHOMP
?
YEEAAAH!
THIS IS NOT WORKING OUT
ANDERSON

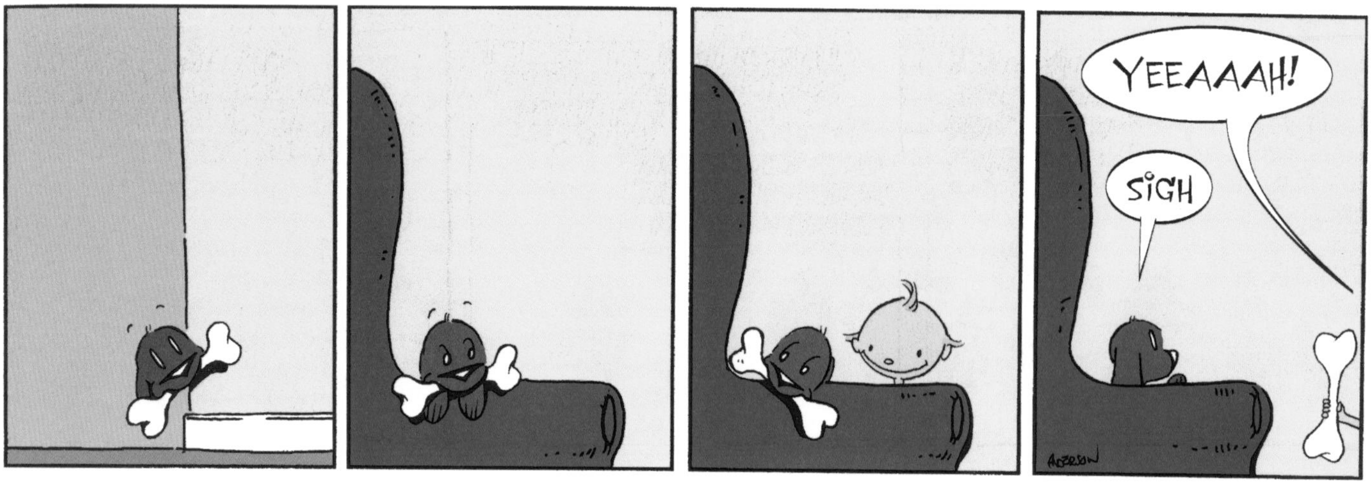
YEEAAAH!
SIGH
ANDERSON

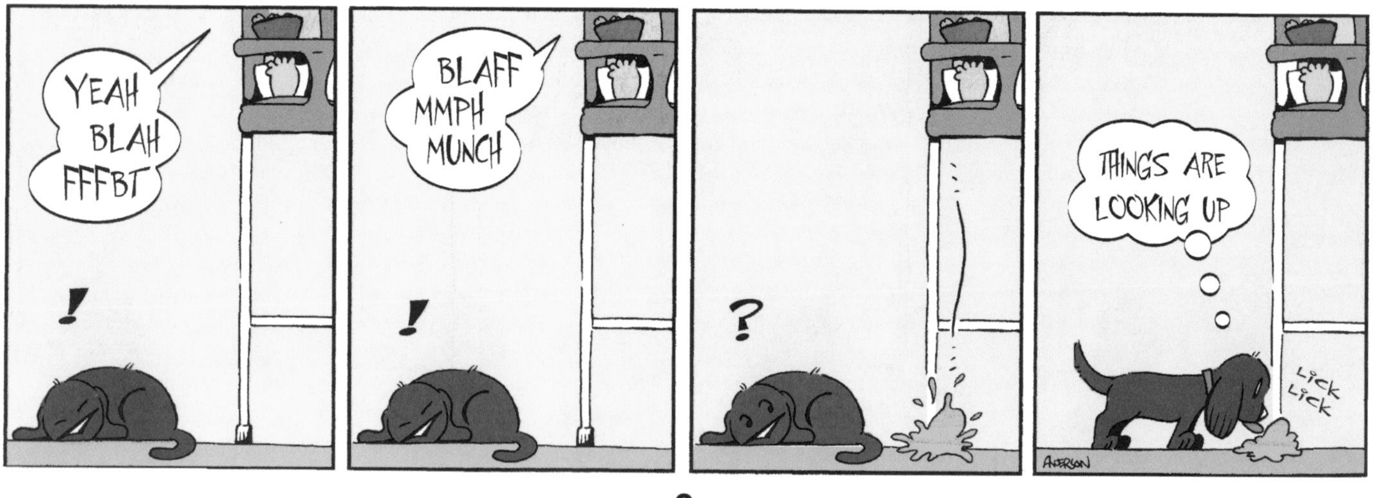
YEAH BLAH FFFBT
!
BLAFF MMPH MUNCH
!
?
THINGS ARE LOOKING UP
LICK LICK
ANDERSON

ZING!
ZING!
ZING!
ZING!
SOPHIE! GO OUTSIDE AND PLAY!
Z

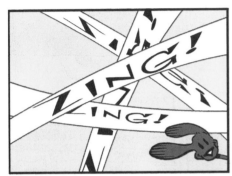

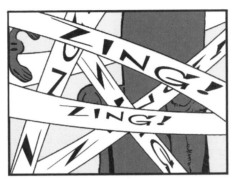

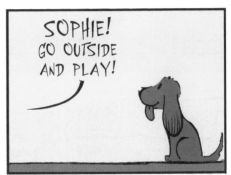

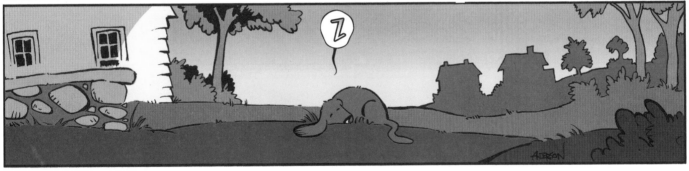

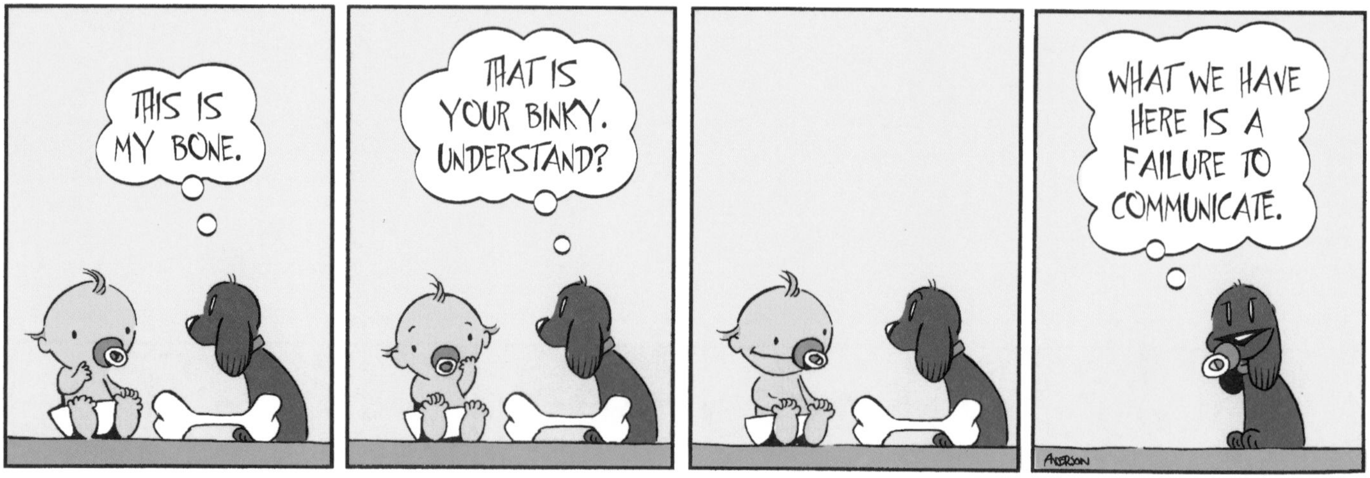
THIS IS MY BONE.
THAT IS YOUR BINKY. UNDERSTAND?
WHAT WE HAVE HERE IS A FAILURE TO COMMUNICATE.
ANDERSON

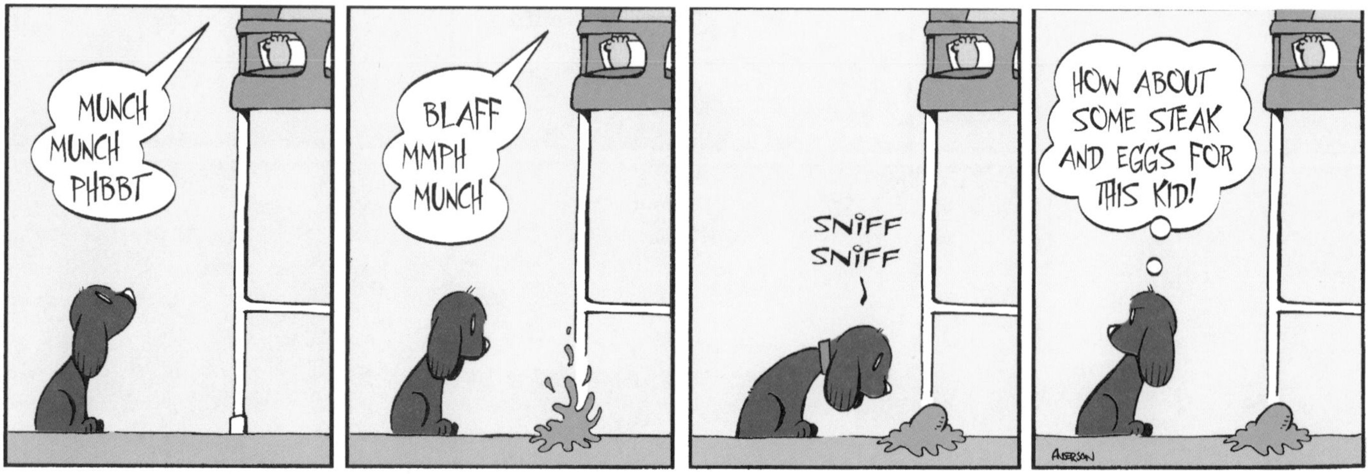
MUNCH MUNCH PHBBT
BLAFF MMPH MUNCH
SNIFF SNIFF
HOW ABOUT SOME STEAK AND EGGS FOR THIS KID!
ANDERSON

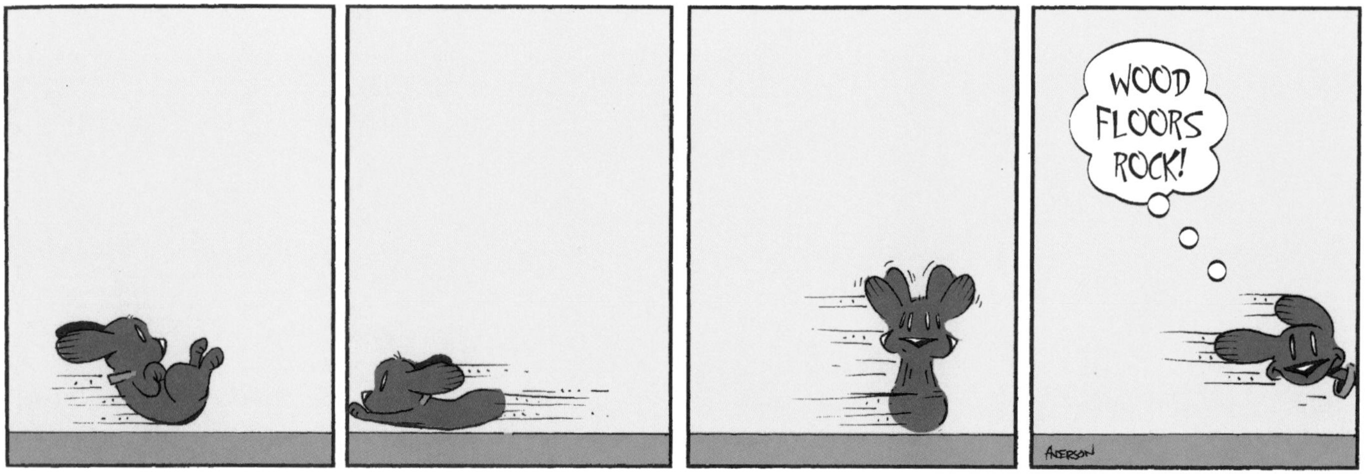
WOOD FLOORS ROCK!
ANDERSON

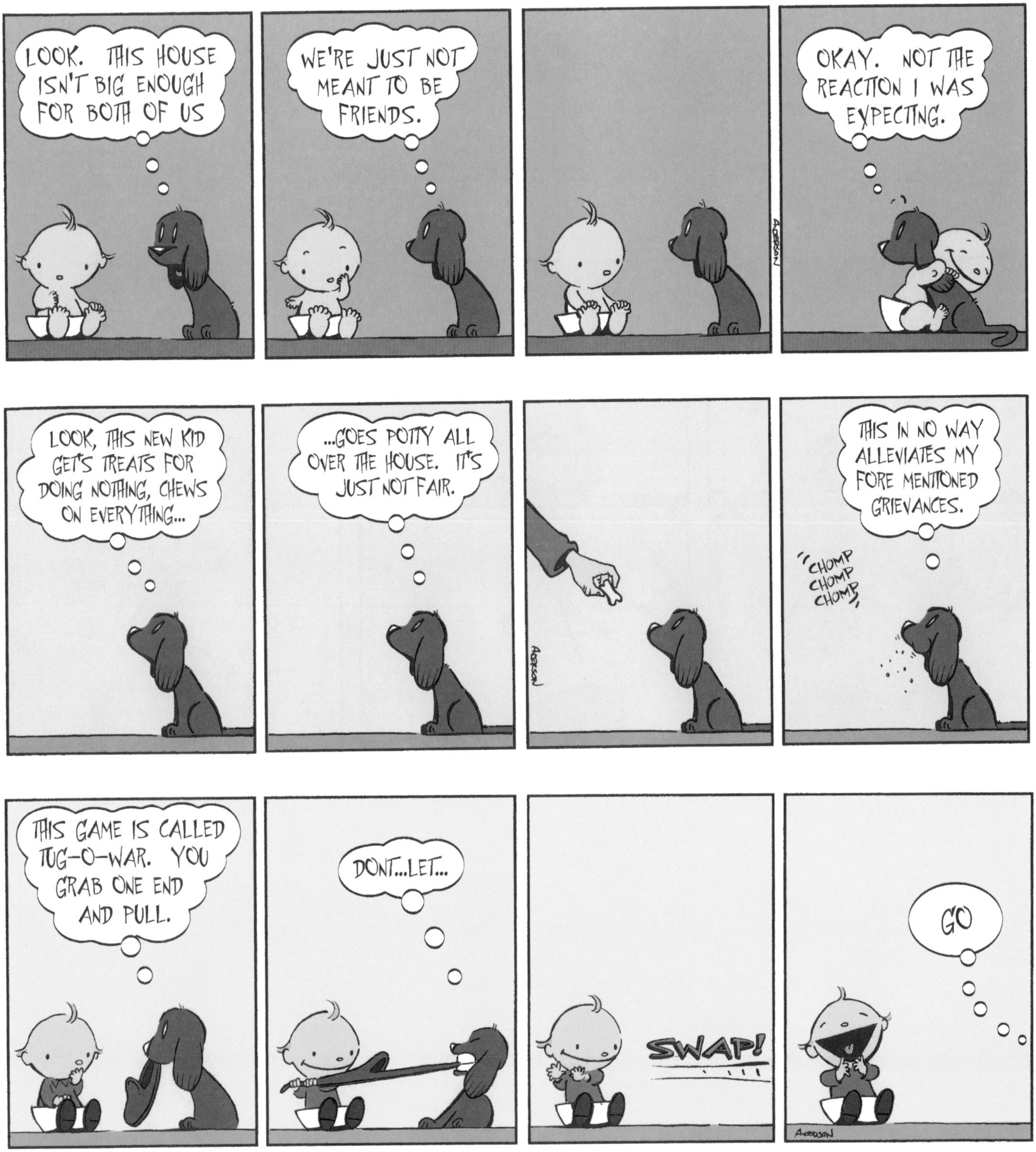
LOOK. THIS HOUSE ISN'T BIG ENOUGH FOR BOTH OF US
WE'RE JUST NOT MEANT TO BE FRIENDS.
OKAY. NOT THE REACTION I WAS EXPECTING.
LOOK, THIS NEW KID GET'S TREATS FOR DOING NOTHING, CHEWS ON EVERYTHING...
...GOES POTTY ALL OVER THE HOUSE. IT'S JUST NOT FAIR.
CHOMP CHOMP CHOMP
THIS IN NO WAY ALLEVIATES MY FORE MENTIONED GRIEVANCES.
THIS GAME IS CALLED TUG-O-WAR. YOU GRAB ONE END AND PULL.
DONT...LET...
SWAP!
GO

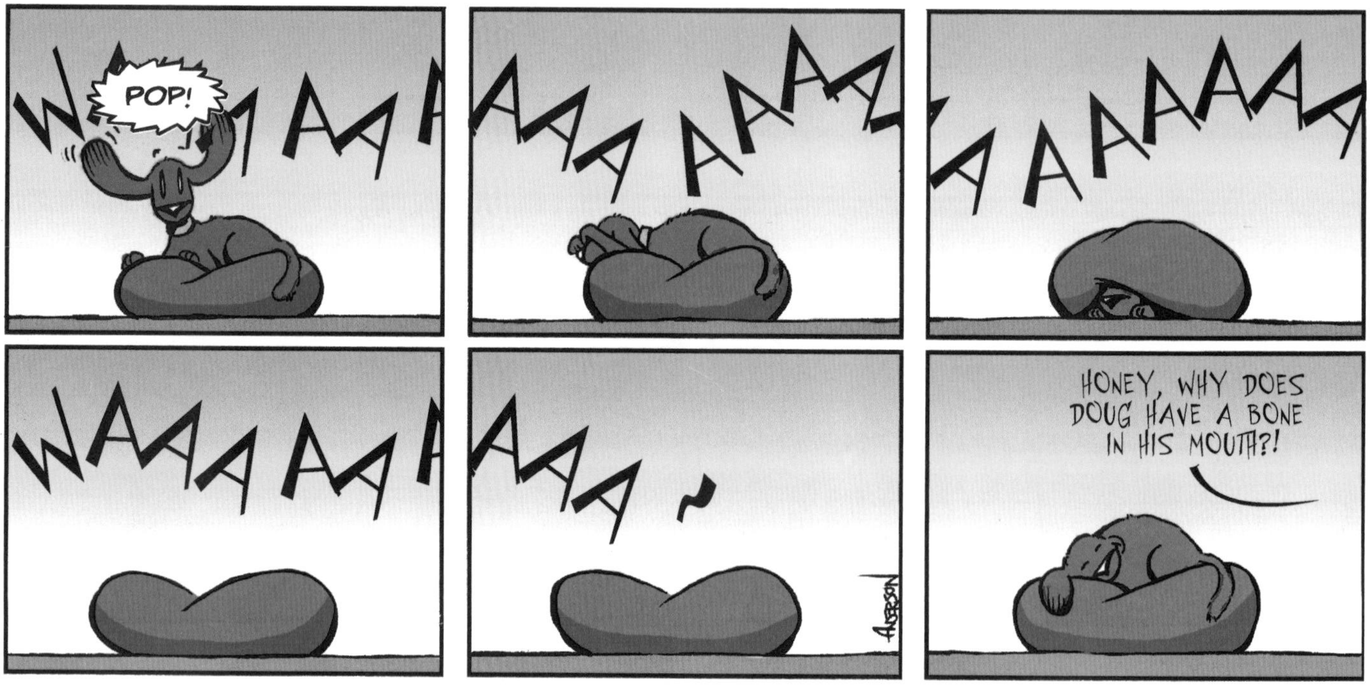
POP!
WAAAAAAAAAAAAAAAAAAAAAAAAAAAAAAAAA
WAAAAAAAAAAAAA ~
HONEY, WHY DOES DOUG HAVE A BONE IN HIS MOUTH?!

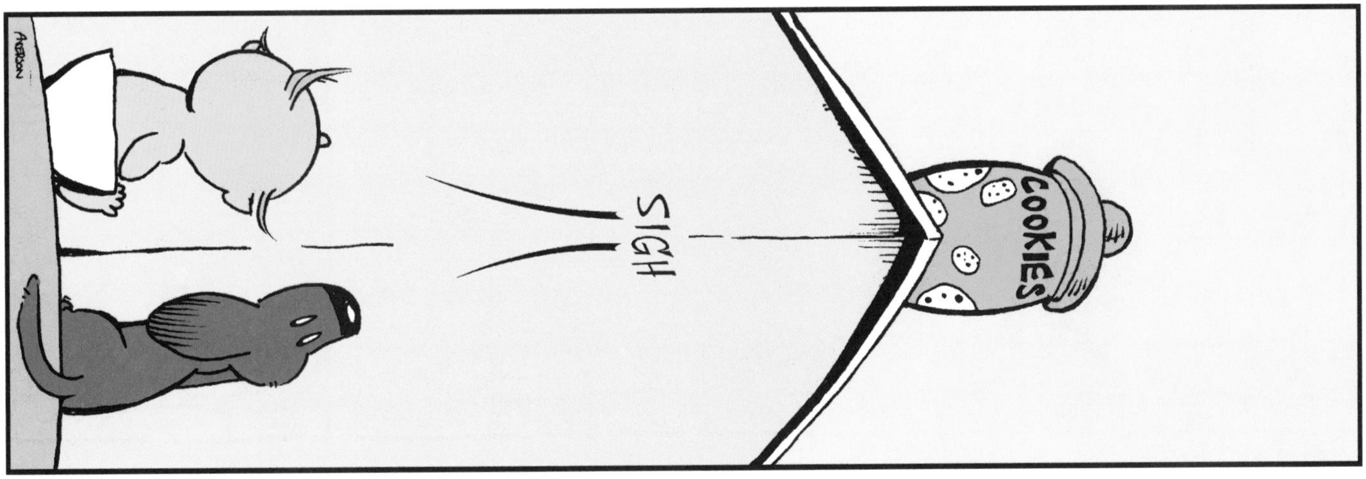
SIGH
COOKIES

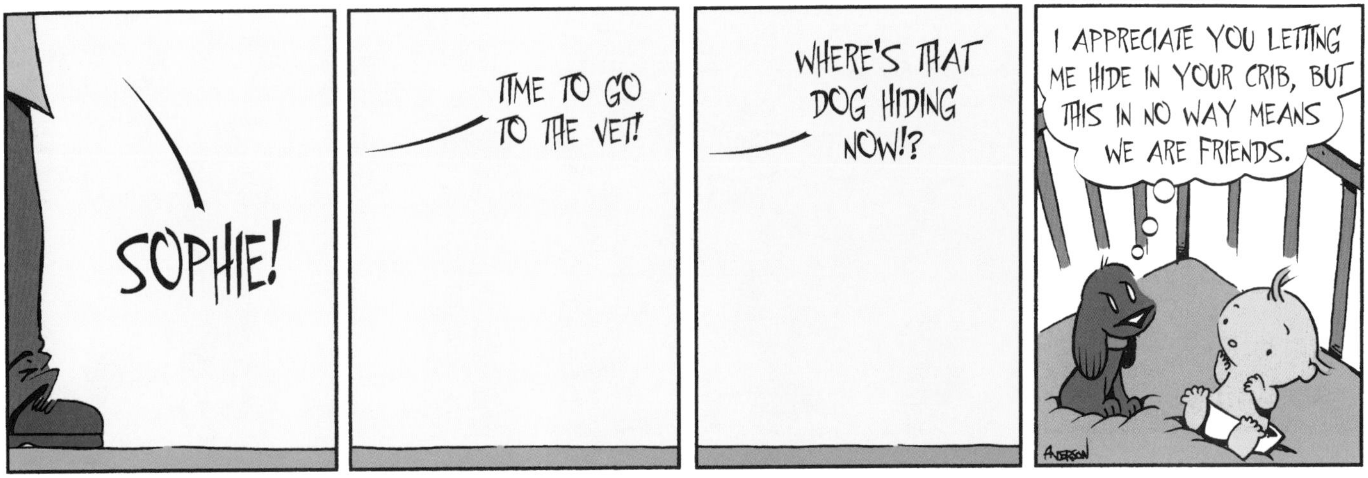
SOPHIE!
TIME TO GO TO THE VET!
WHERE'S THAT DOG HIDING NOW!?
I APPRECIATE YOU LETTING ME HIDE IN YOUR CRIB, BUT THIS IN NO WAY MEANS WE ARE FRIENDS.

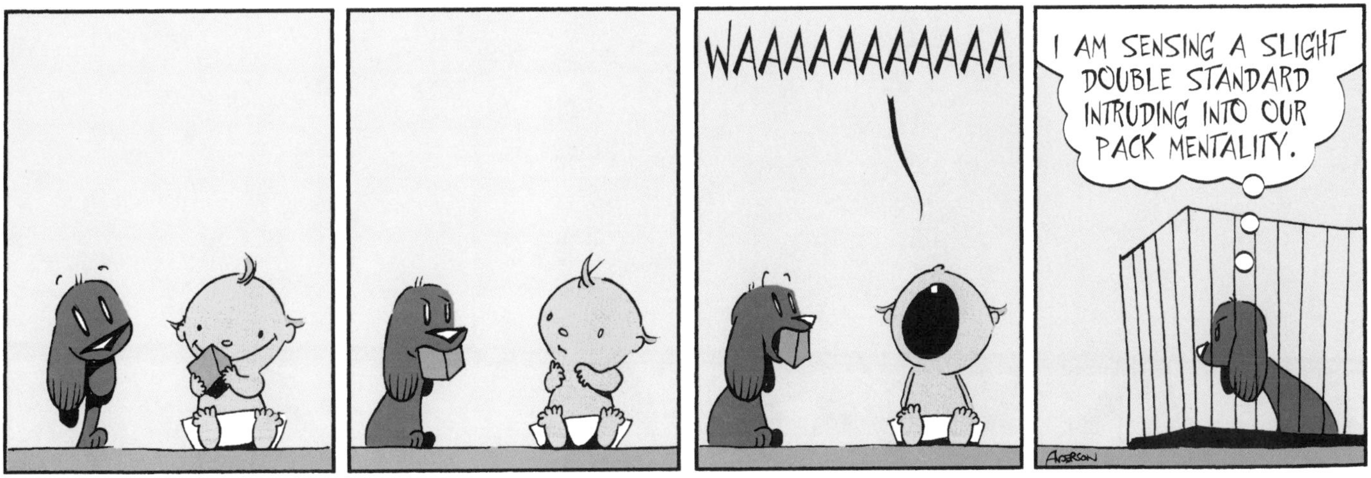
WAAAAAAAAAA
I AM SENSING A SLIGHT DOUBLE STANDARD INTRUDING INTO OUR PACK MENTALITY.

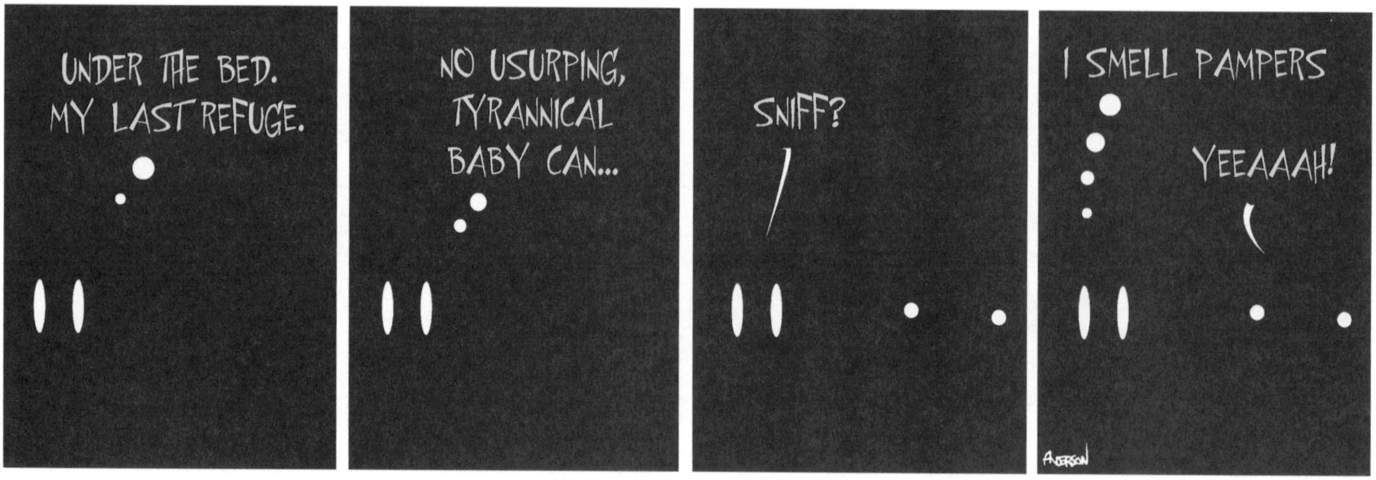
UNDER THE BED. MY LAST REFUGE.
NO USURPING, TYRANNICAL BABY CAN...
SNIFF?
I SMELL PAMPERS
YEEAAAH!
ANDERSON

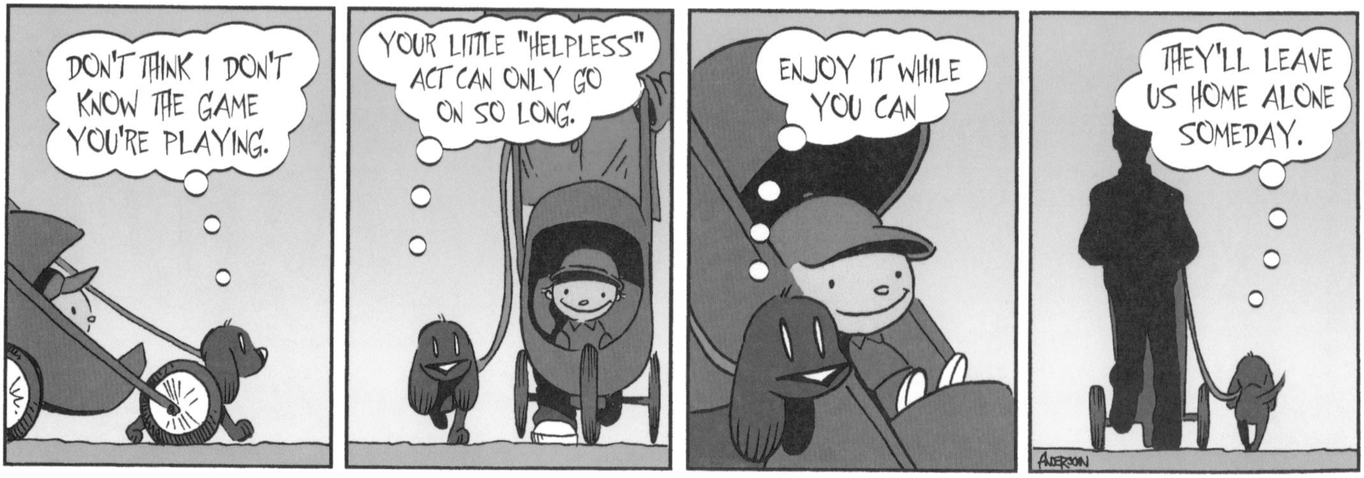
DON'T THINK I DON'T KNOW THE GAME YOU'RE PLAYING.
YOUR LITTLE "HELPLESS" ACT CAN ONLY GO ON SO LONG.
ENJOY IT WHILE YOU CAN
THEY'LL LEAVE US HOME ALONE SOMEDAY.
ANDERSON

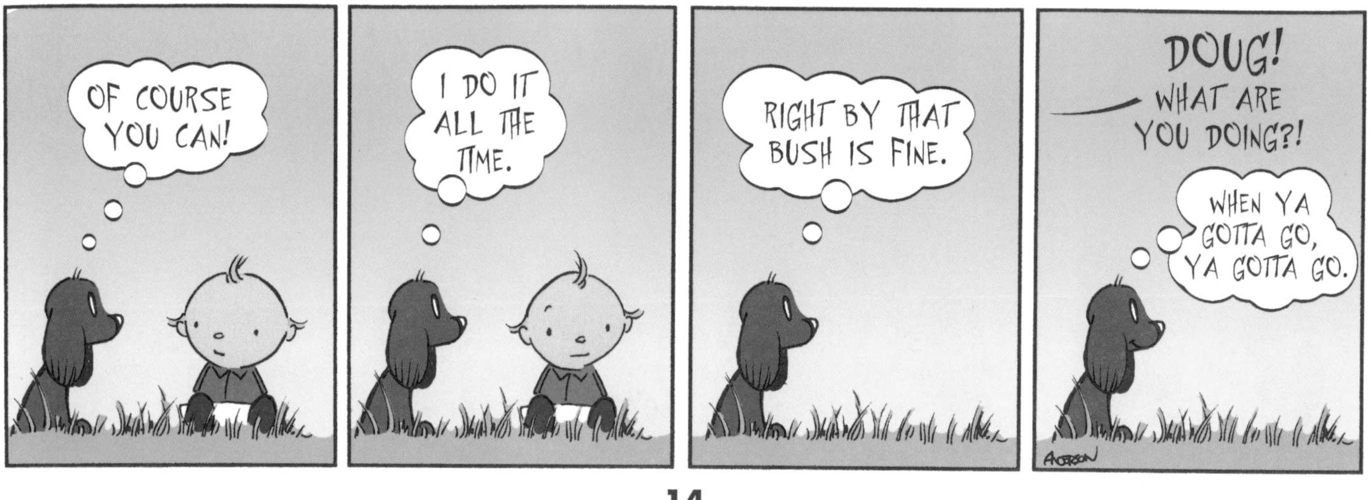
OF COURSE YOU CAN!
I DO IT ALL THE TIME.
RIGHT BY THAT BUSH IS FINE.
DOUG! WHAT ARE YOU DOING?!
WHEN YA GOTTA GO, YA GOTTA GO.
ANDERSON

WHAT'S SO SPECIAL ABOUT BABIES?!
THEY JUST LIE AROUND ALL DAY
CAN'T FETCH, CAN'T PLAY CHASE.
BABY'S DON'T HAVE ONE REDEEMABLE QUALITY!
SMOOOCH!
SHEESH! JUST WHEN YOU THINK YOU KNOW SOMEONE!

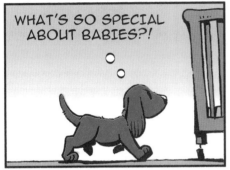

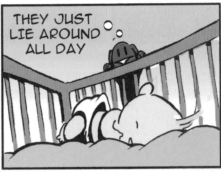

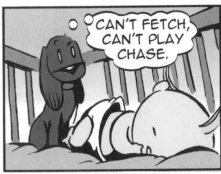

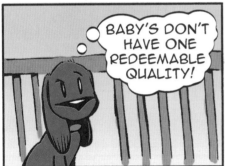

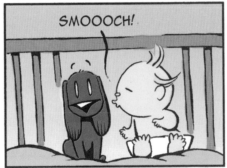

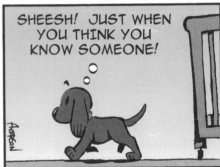

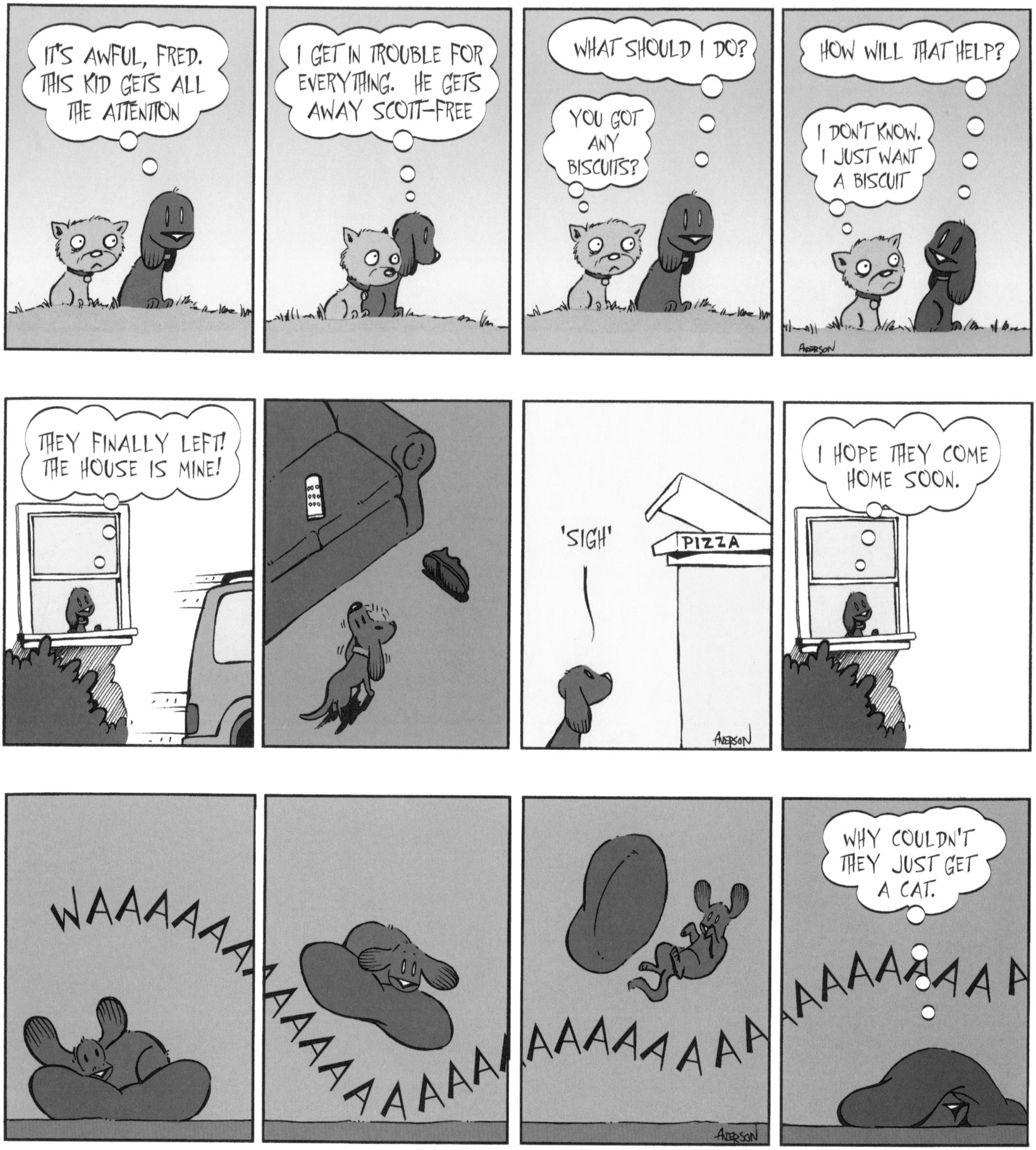
IT'S AWFUL, FRED. THIS KID GETS ALL THE ATTENTION
I GET IN TROUBLE FOR EVERYTHING. HE GETS AWAY SCOTT-FREE
WHAT SHOULD I DO?
YOU GOT ANY BISCUITS?
HOW WILL THAT HELP?
I DON'T KNOW. I JUST WANT A BISCUIT
ANDERSON
THEY FINALLY LEFT! THE HOUSE IS MINE!
'SIGH'
PIZZA
ANDERSON
I HOPE THEY COME HOME SOON.
WAAAAAAAAAAAAAAAAAAAAAAAAAAAAAAAAAA
WHY COULDN'T THEY JUST GET A CAT.
ANDERSON

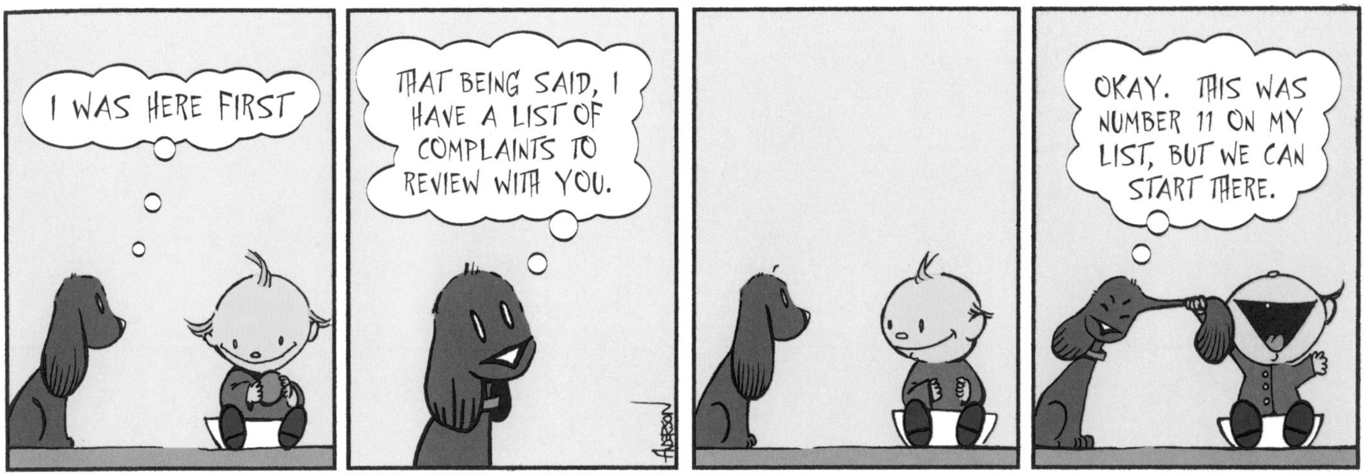
I WAS HERE FIRST
THAT BEING SAID, I HAVE A LIST OF COMPLAINTS TO REVIEW WITH YOU.
OKAY. THIS WAS NUMBER 11 ON MY LIST, BUT WE CAN START THERE.

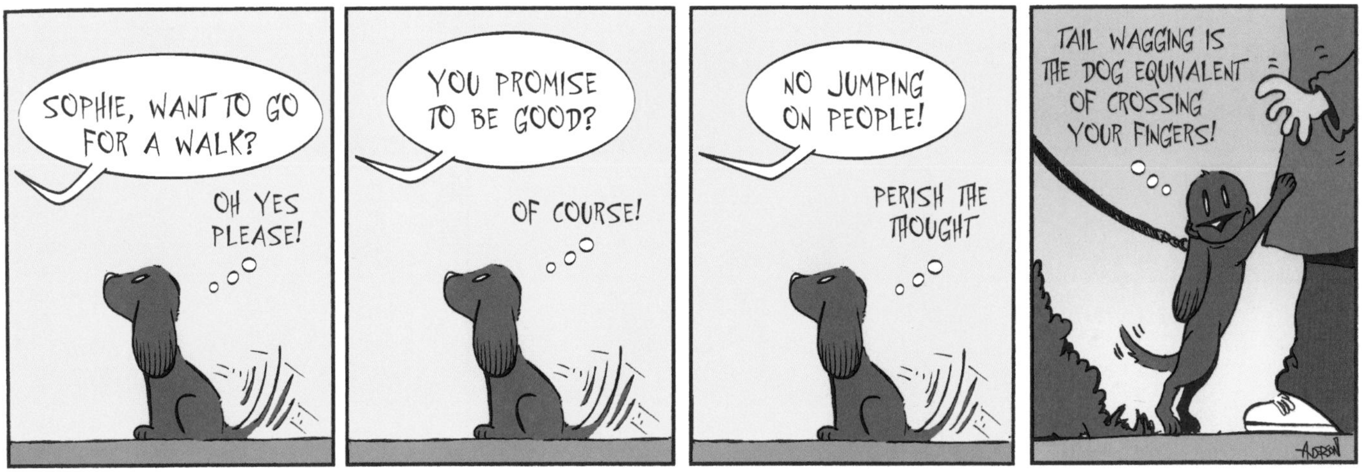
SOPHIE, WANT TO GO FOR A WALK?
OH YES PLEASE!
YOU PROMISE TO BE GOOD?
OF COURSE!
NO JUMPING ON PEOPLE!
PERISH THE THOUGHT
TAIL WAGGING IS THE DOG EQUIVALENT OF CROSSING YOUR FINGERS!

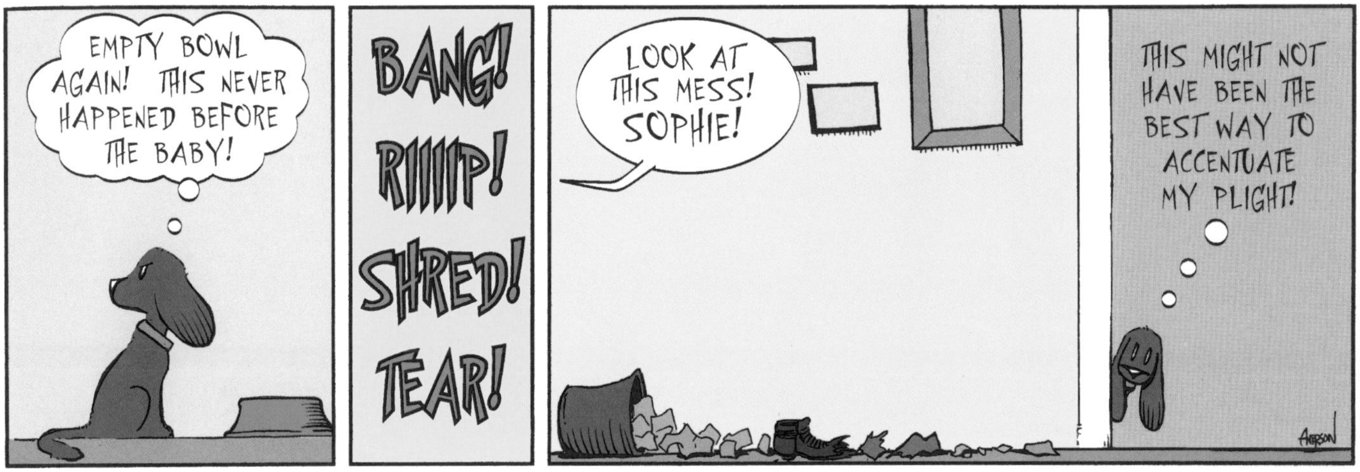
EMPTY BOWL AGAIN! THIS NEVER HAPPENED BEFORE THE BABY!
BANG!
RIIIIP!
SHRED!
TEAR!
LOOK AT THIS MESS! SOPHIE!
THIS MIGHT NOT HAVE BEEN THE BEST WAY TO ACCENTUATE MY PLIGHT!

SOPHIE, SIT!
ROLLOVER.
STAND UP!
LIE DOWN.
GOOD GIRL!
IT'S A LOT OF WORK, BUT THOSE TREATS SURE ARE WORTH IT!
MUNCH! MUNCH! MUNCH!

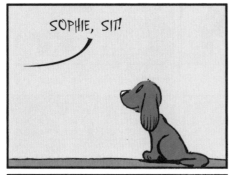

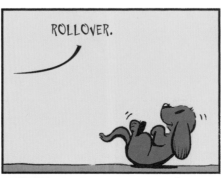

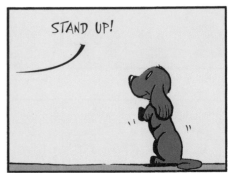

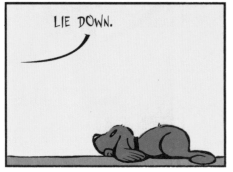

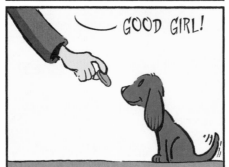

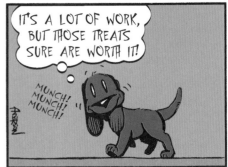

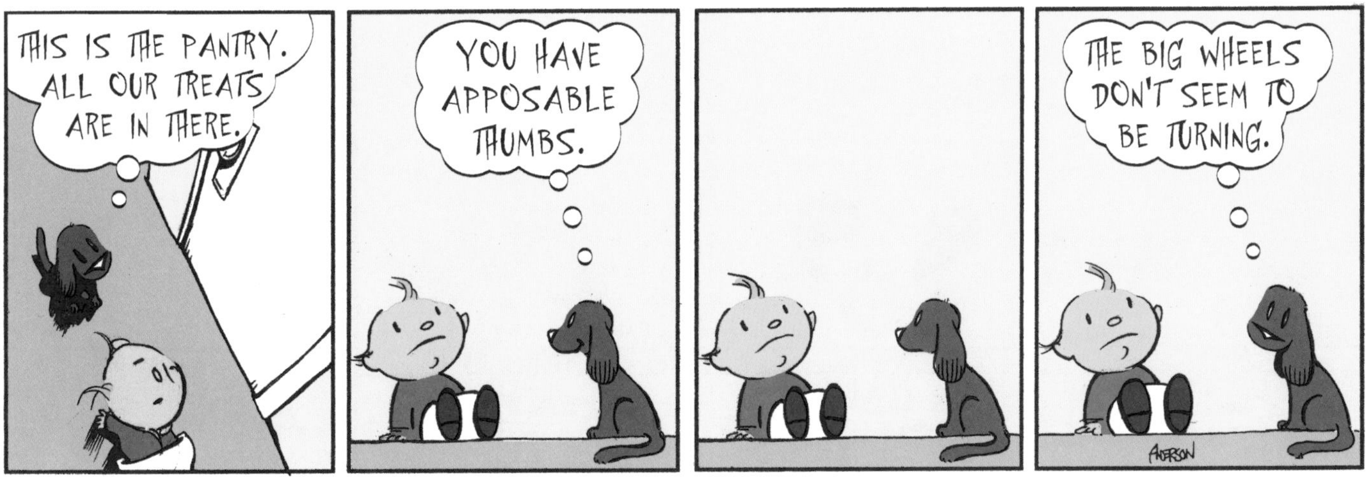
THIS IS THE PANTRY. ALL OUR TREATS ARE IN THERE.
YOU HAVE APPOSABLE THUMBS.
THE BIG WHEELS DON'T SEEM TO BE TURNING.
ANDERSON

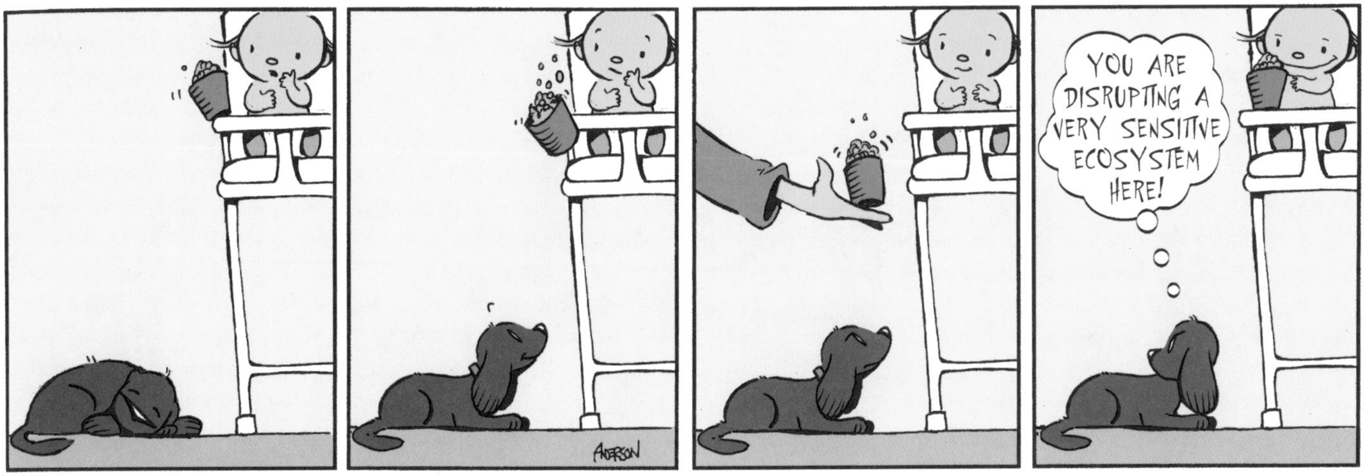
ANDERSON
YOU ARE DISRUPTING A VERY SENSITIVE ECOSYSTEM HERE!

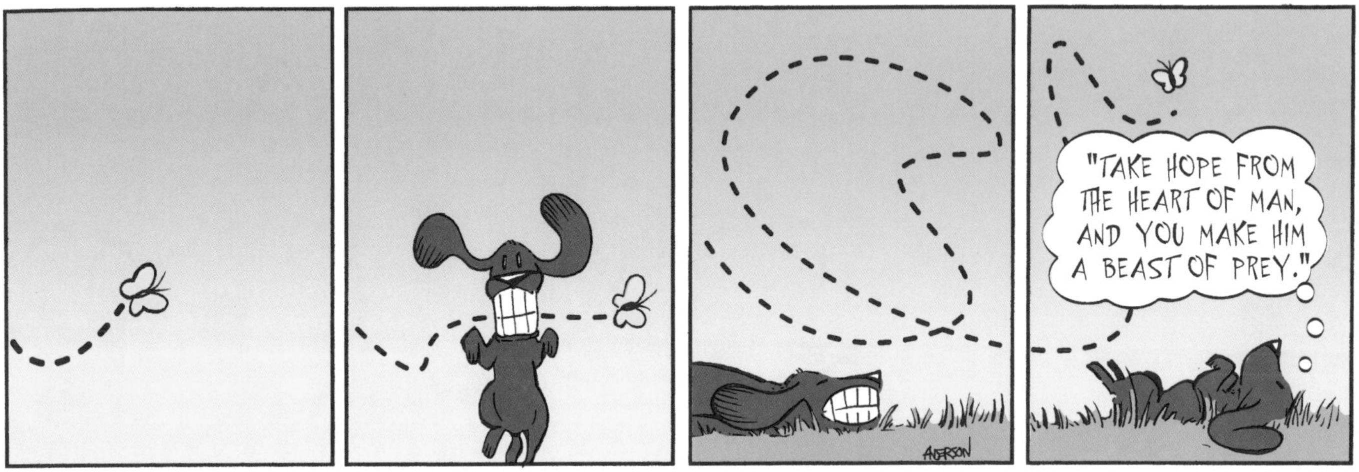
ANDERSON
"TAKE HOPE FROM THE HEART OF MAN, AND YOU MAKE HIM A BEAST OF PREY."

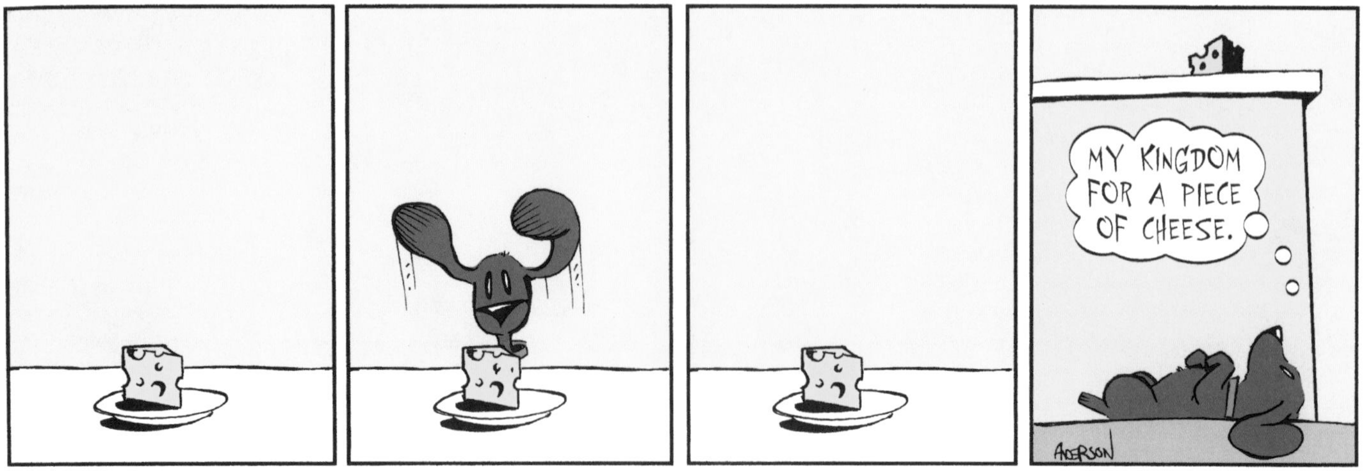
MY KINGDOM FOR A PIECE OF CHEESE.
ANDERSON

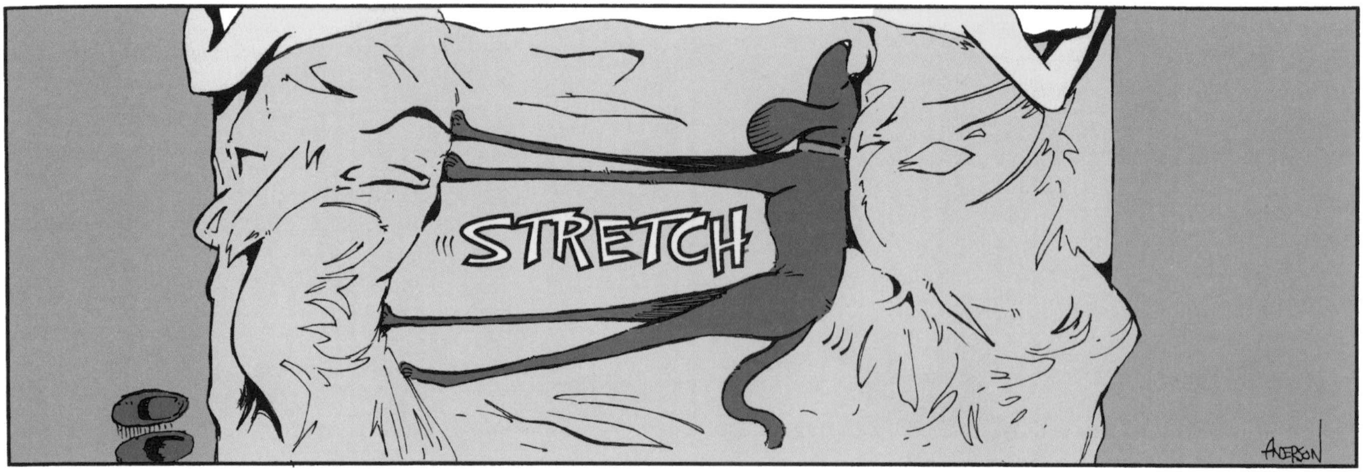
STRETCH
ANDERSON

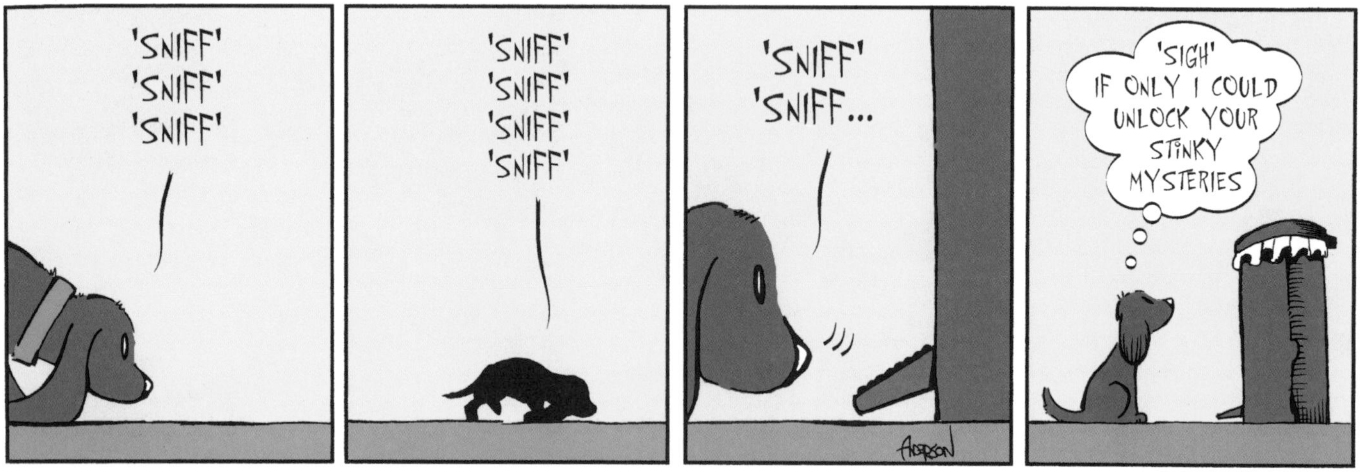
'SNIFF' 'SNIFF' 'SNIFF'
'SNIFF' 'SNIFF' 'SNIFF' 'SNIFF'
'SNIFF' 'SNIFF...
ANDERSON
'SIGH' IF ONLY I COULD UNLOCK YOUR STINKY MYSTERIES

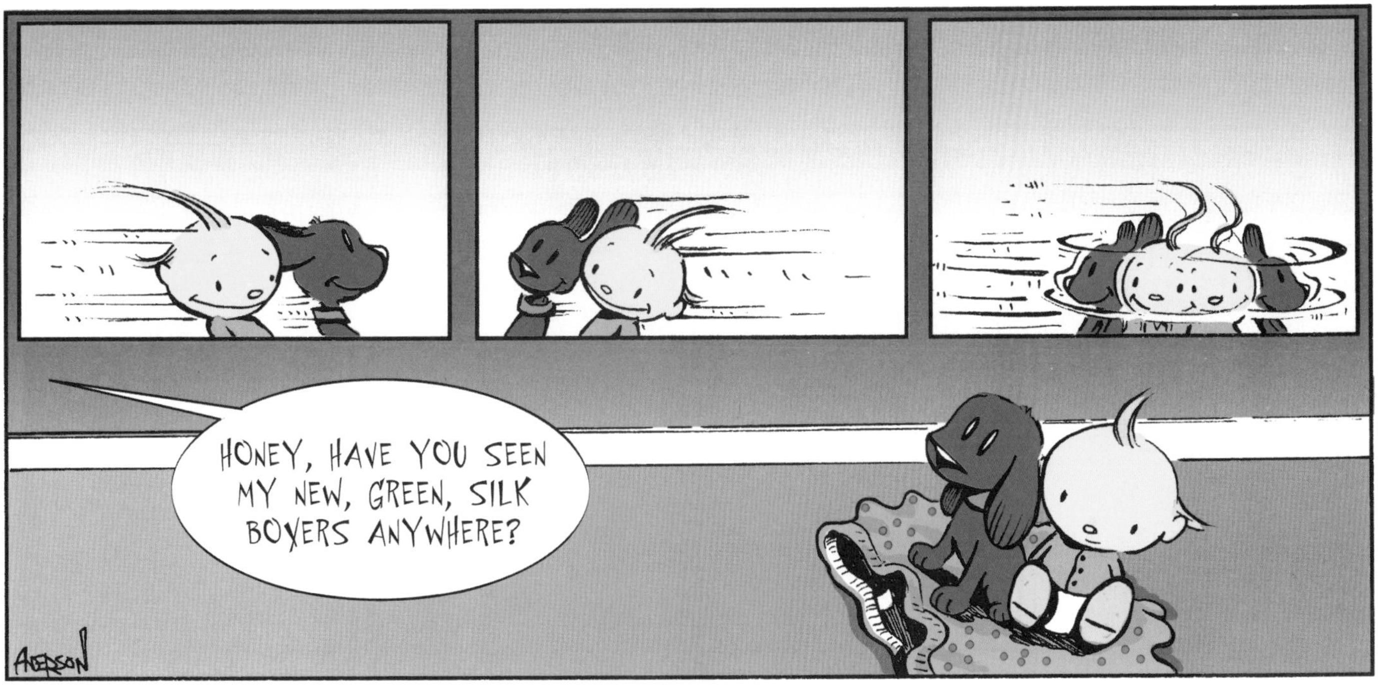
HONEY, HAVE YOU SEEN MY NEW, GREEN, SILK BOXERS ANYWHERE?
ANDERSON

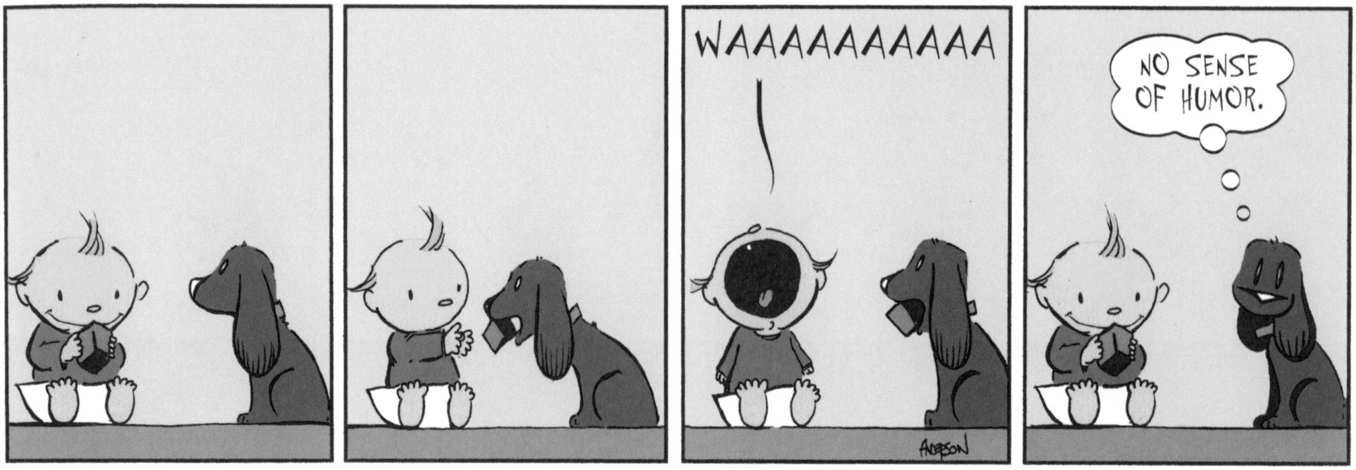
WAAAAAAAAAA
NO SENSE OF HUMOR.

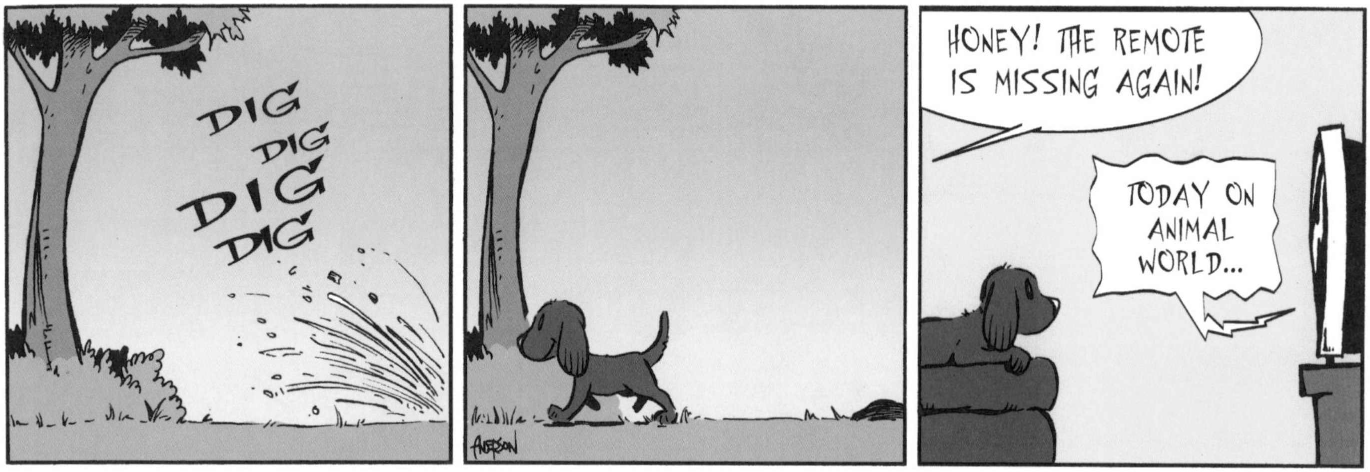
DIG DIG DIG DIG
HONEY! THE REMOTE IS MISSING AGAIN!
TODAY ON ANIMAL WORLD...

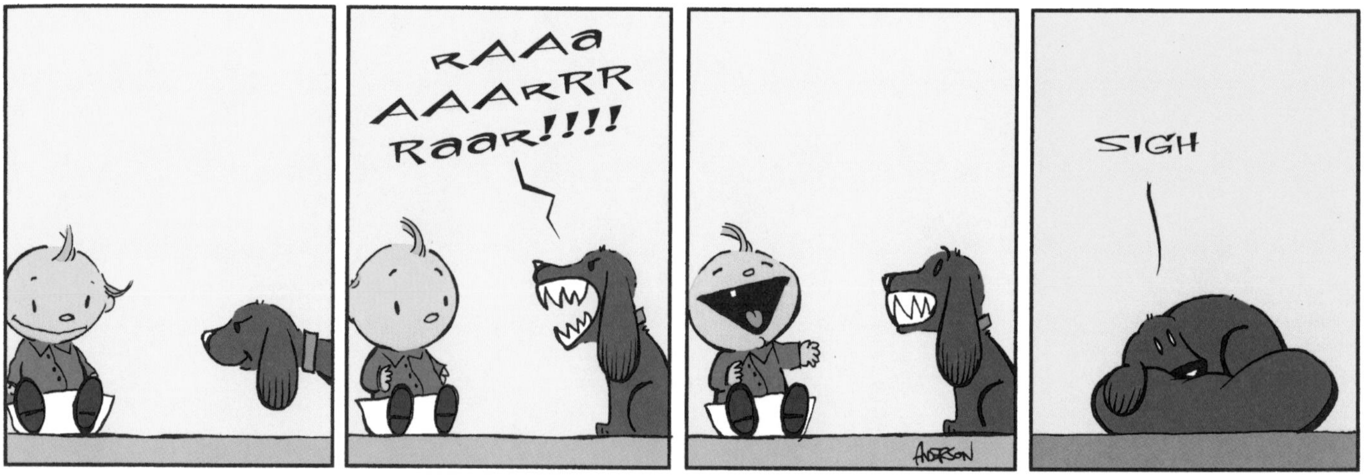
RAAa AAARRR Raar!!!!
SIGH

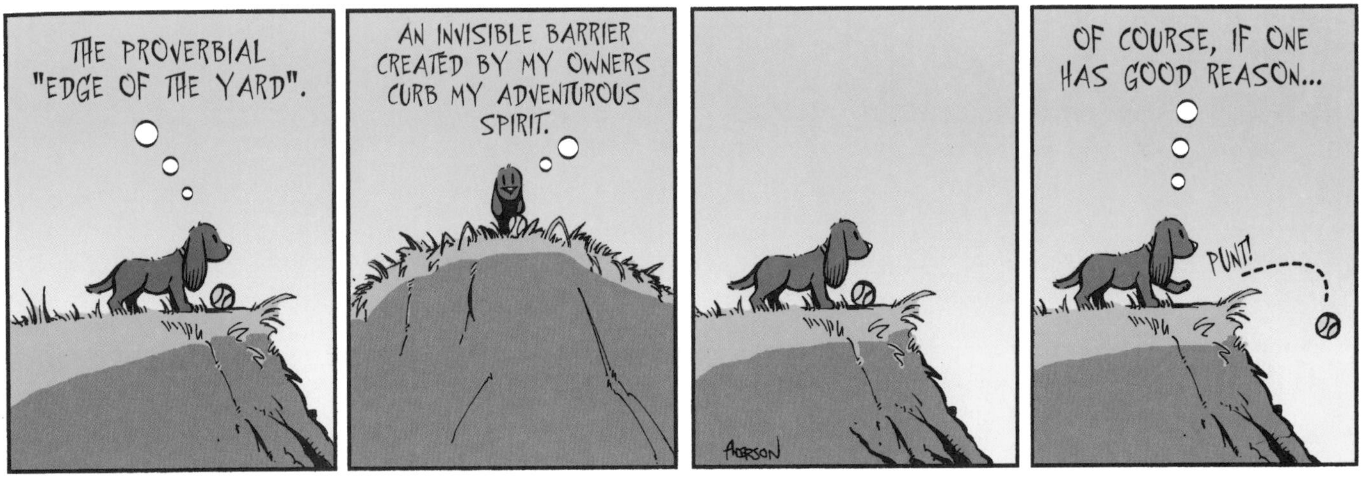
THE PROVERBIAL "EDGE OF THE YARD".
AN INVISIBLE BARRIER CREATED BY MY OWNERS CURB MY ADVENTUROUS SPIRIT.
OF COURSE, IF ONE HAS GOOD REASON...
PUNT!

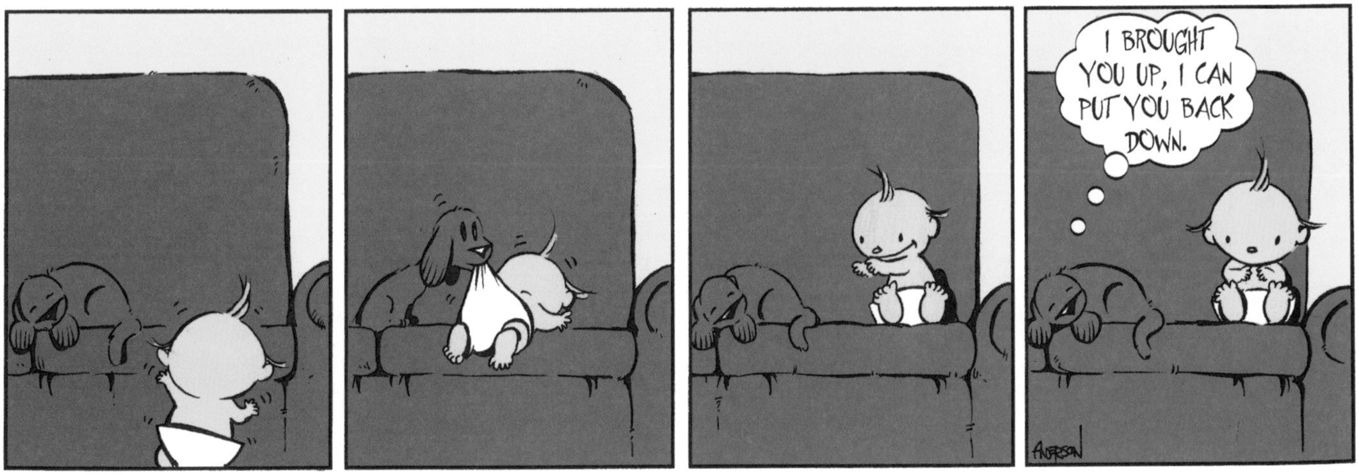
I BROUGHT YOU UP, I CAN PUT YOU BACK DOWN.

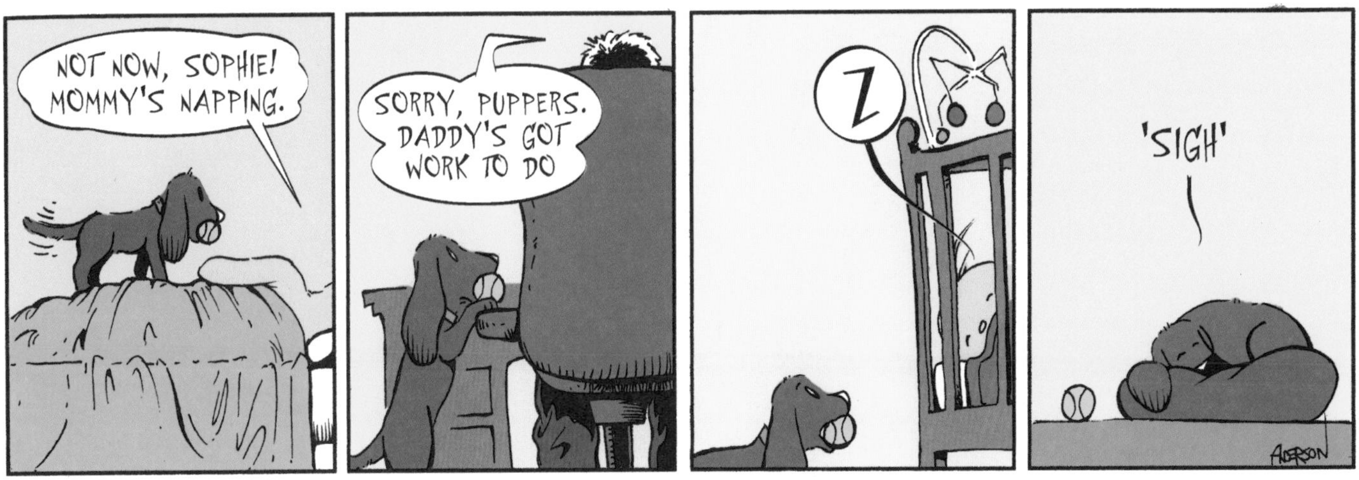
NOT NOW, SOPHIE! MOMMY'S NAPPING.
SORRY, PUPPERS. DADDY'S GOT WORK TO DO
Z
'SIGH'

THIS IS THE PERFECT HIDING SPOT TO CATCH SANTA RED-HANDED!
WE'LL NEED TO STAY VIGILANT!
NO SLEEPING ON DUTY! HE COULD BE ANYWHERE!
NOTHING CAN STOP US FROM NAILING THAT OVER-SIZED ELF!
Z
ANDERSON

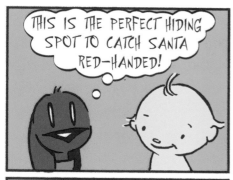

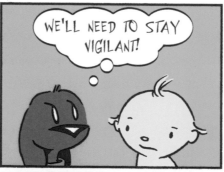

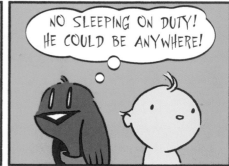

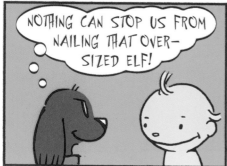

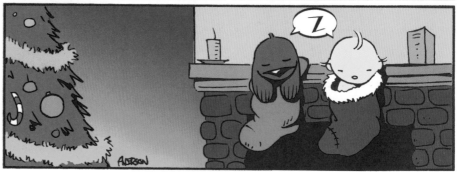

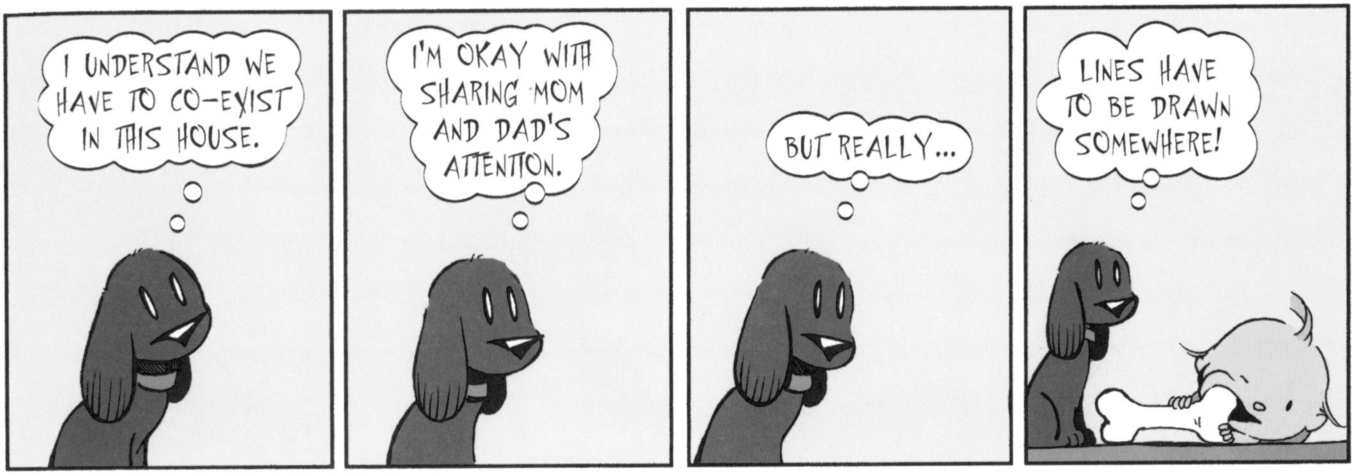
I UNDERSTAND WE HAVE TO CO-EXIST IN THIS HOUSE.
I'M OKAY WITH SHARING MOM AND DAD'S ATTENTION.
BUT REALLY...
LINES HAVE TO BE DRAWN SOMEWHERE!

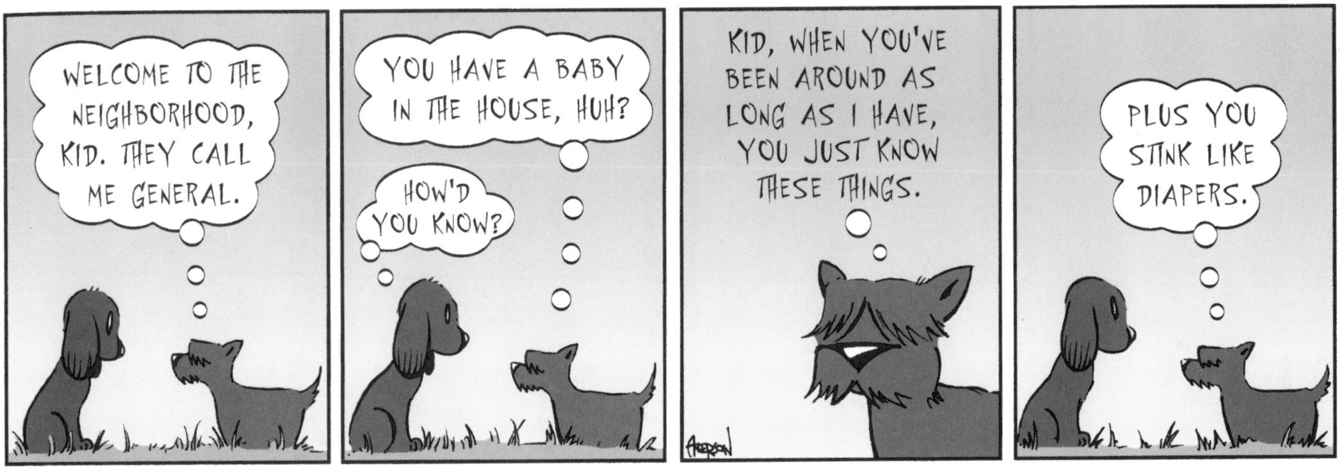
WELCOME TO THE NEIGHBORHOOD, KID. THEY CALL ME GENERAL.
YOU HAVE A BABY IN THE HOUSE, HUH?
HOW'D YOU KNOW?
KID, WHEN YOU'VE BEEN AROUND AS LONG AS I HAVE, YOU JUST KNOW THESE THINGS.
PLUS YOU STINK LIKE DIAPERS.

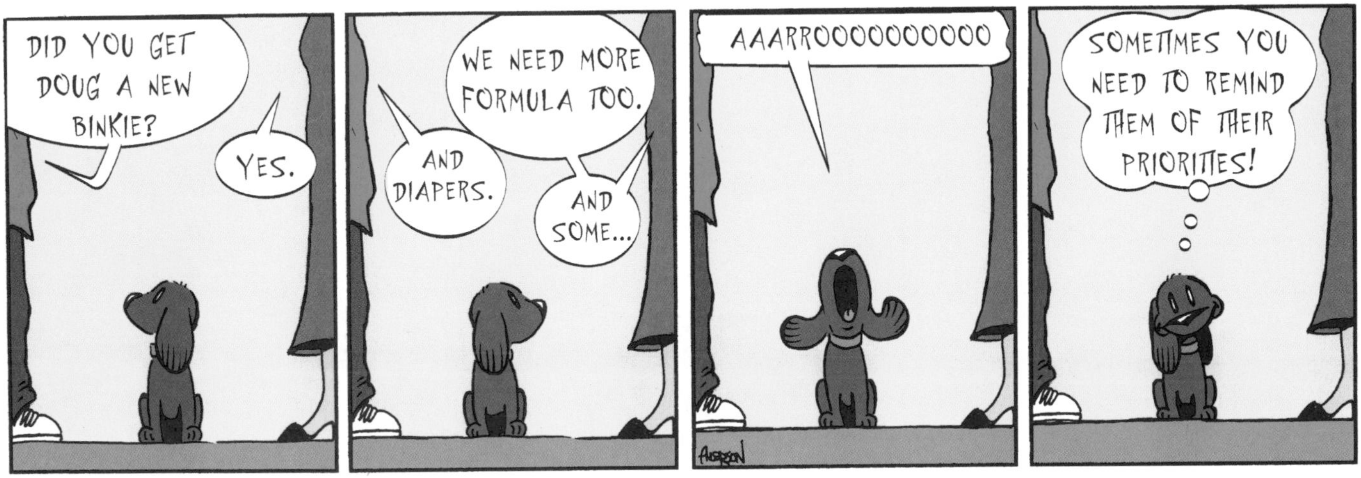
DID YOU GET DOUG A NEW BINKIE?
YES.
WE NEED MORE FORMULA TOO.
AND DIAPERS.
AND SOME...
AAARROOOOOOOOOO
SOMETIMES YOU NEED TO REMIND THEM OF THEIR PRIORITIES!

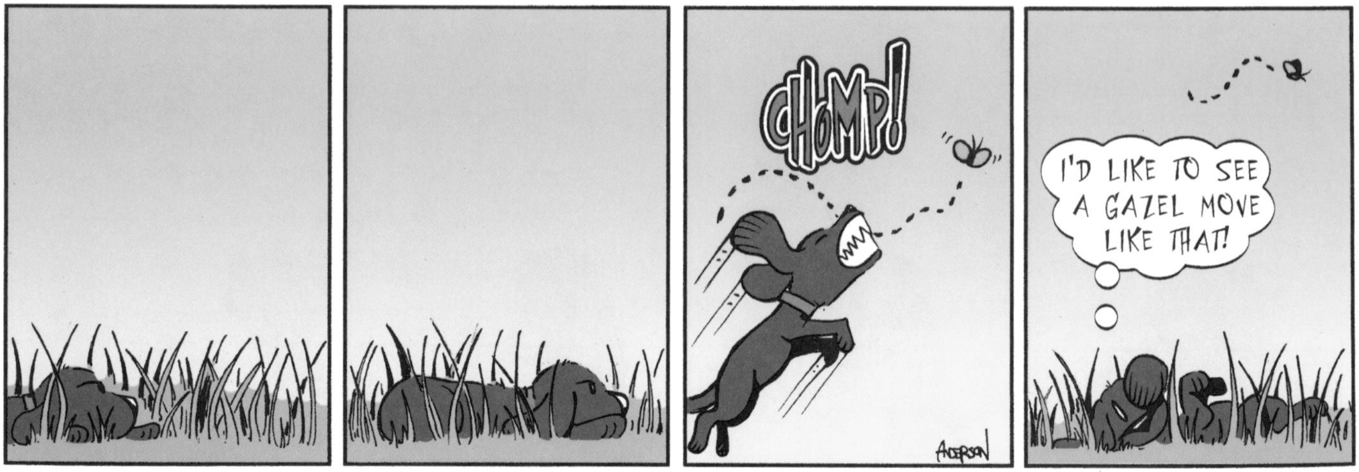
CHOMP!
I'D LIKE TO SEE A GAZEL MOVE LIKE THAT!

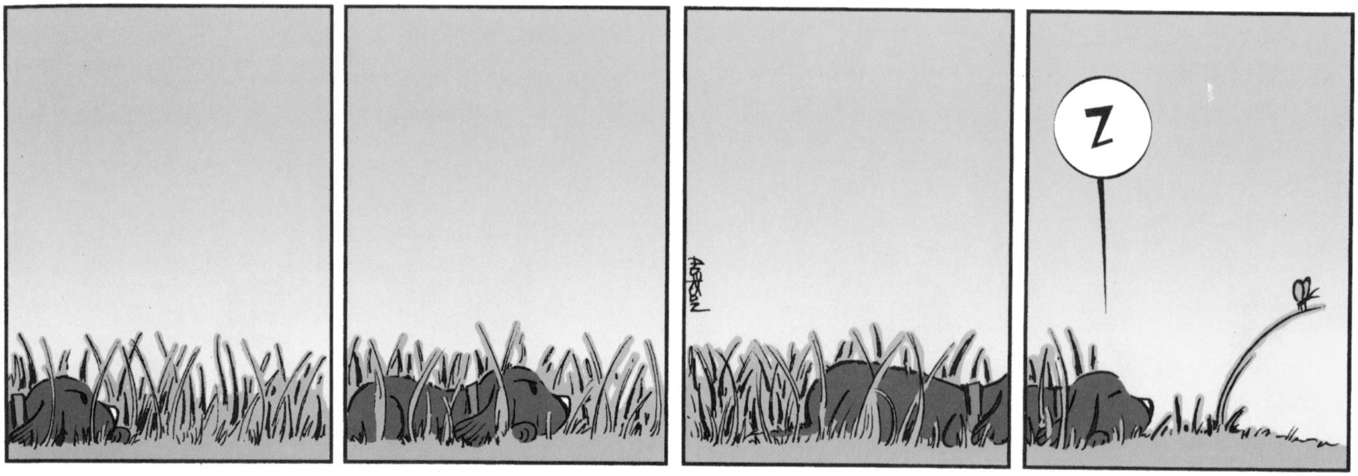
Z

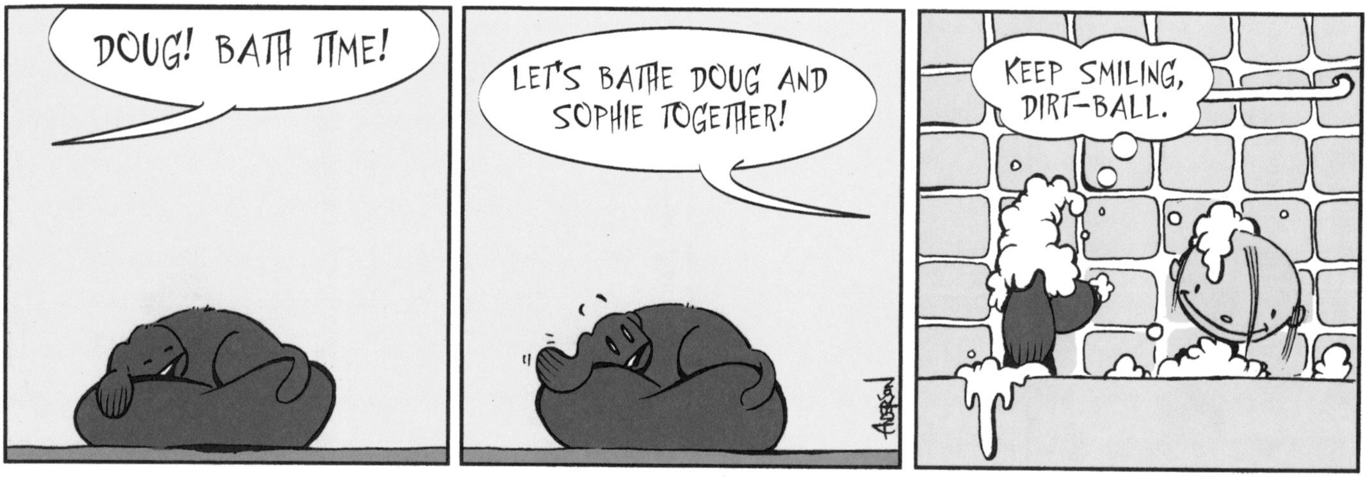
DOUG! BATH TIME!
LET'S BATHE DOUG AND SOPHIE TOGETHER!
KEEP SMILING, DIRT-BALL.

THEY'RE NOT IN HERE.
NOTHING.
ANY LUCK?
TOYS
DAD SAID TO FIND THEM, BUT I DON'T SEE OUR PATIENCE ANYWHERE.

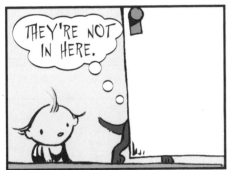

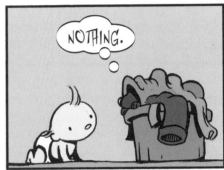

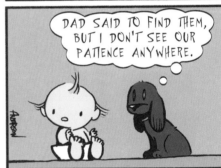

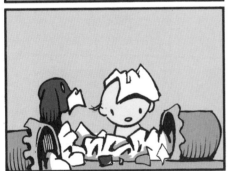

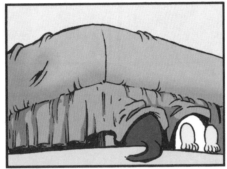

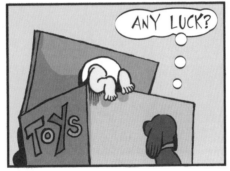

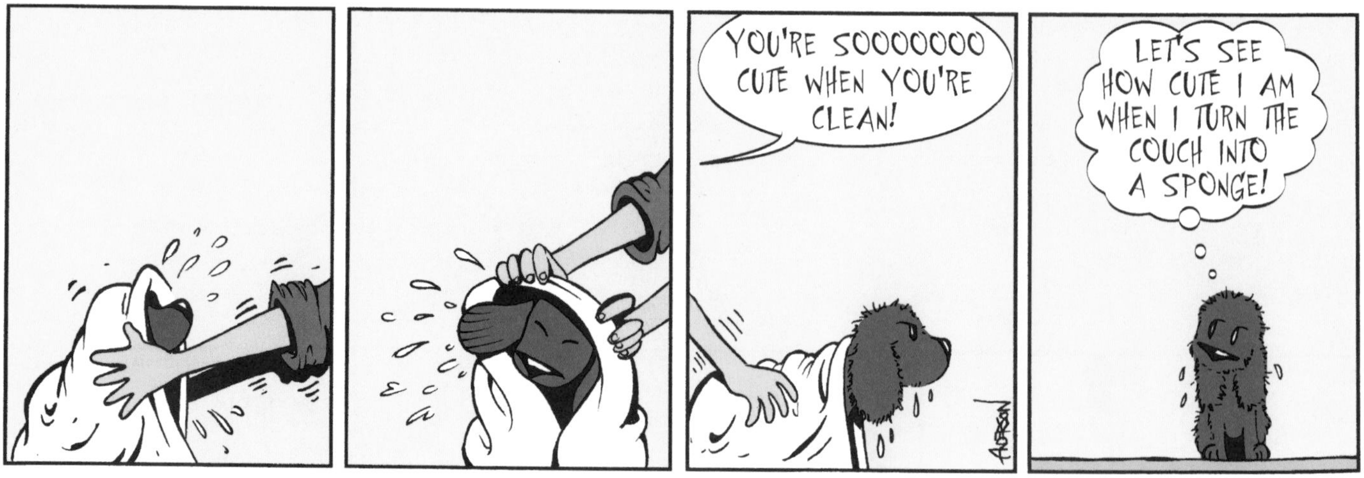
YOU'RE SOOOOOOO CUTE WHEN YOU'RE CLEAN!
LET'S SEE HOW CUTE I AM WHEN I TURN THE COUCH INTO A SPONGE!

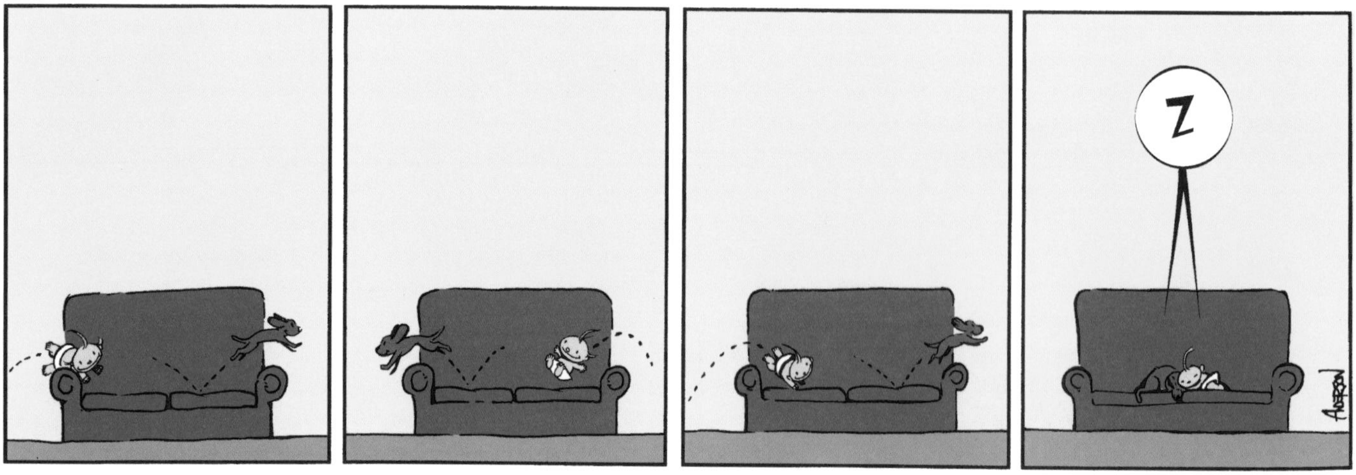
Z

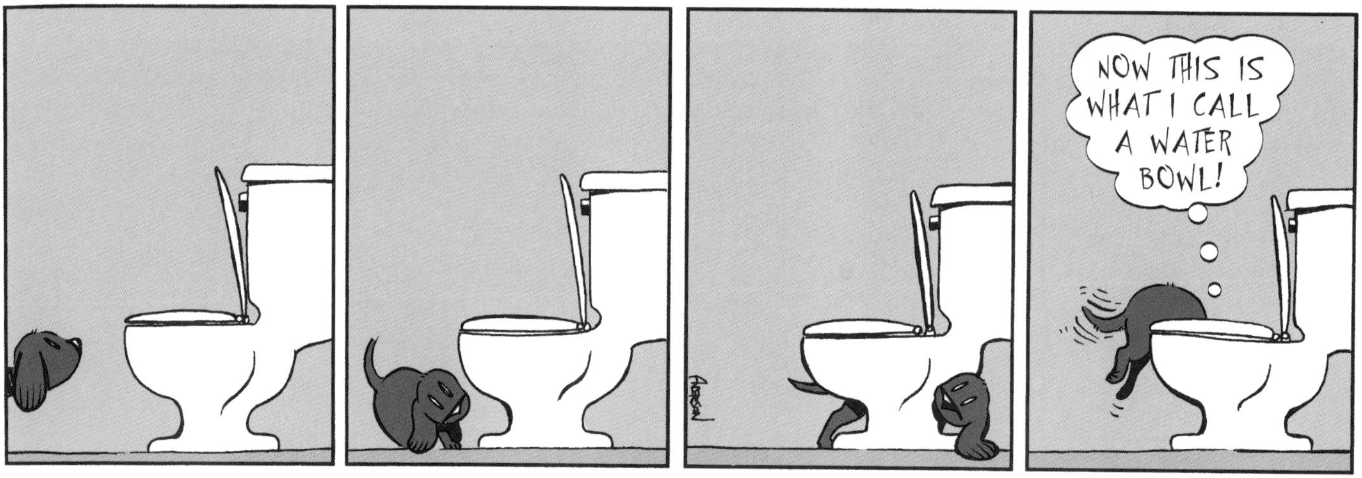
NOW THIS IS WHAT I CALL A WATER BOWL!

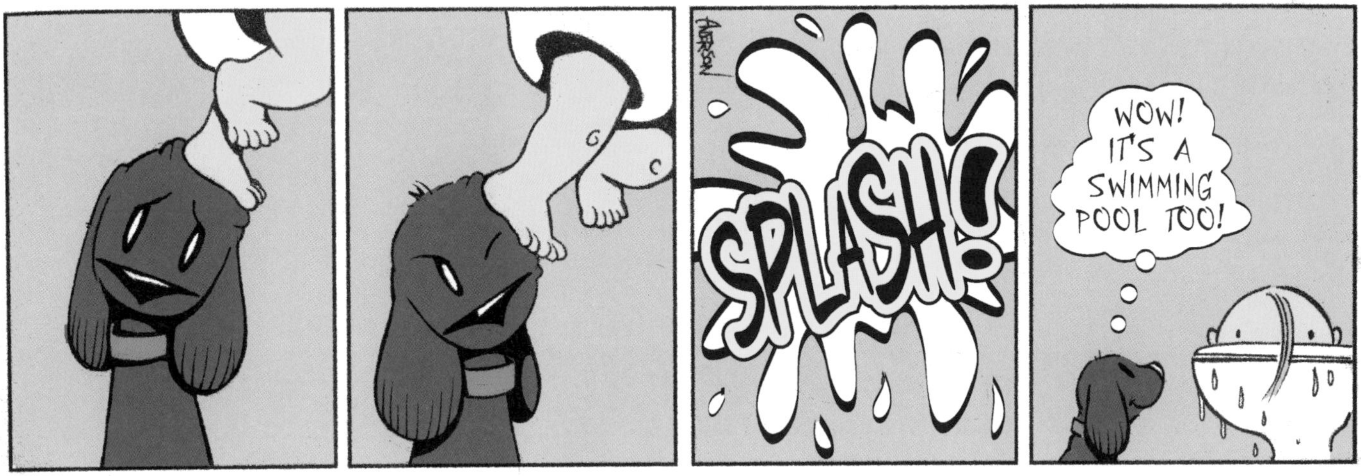
SPLASH!
WOW! IT'S A SWIMMING POOL TOO!

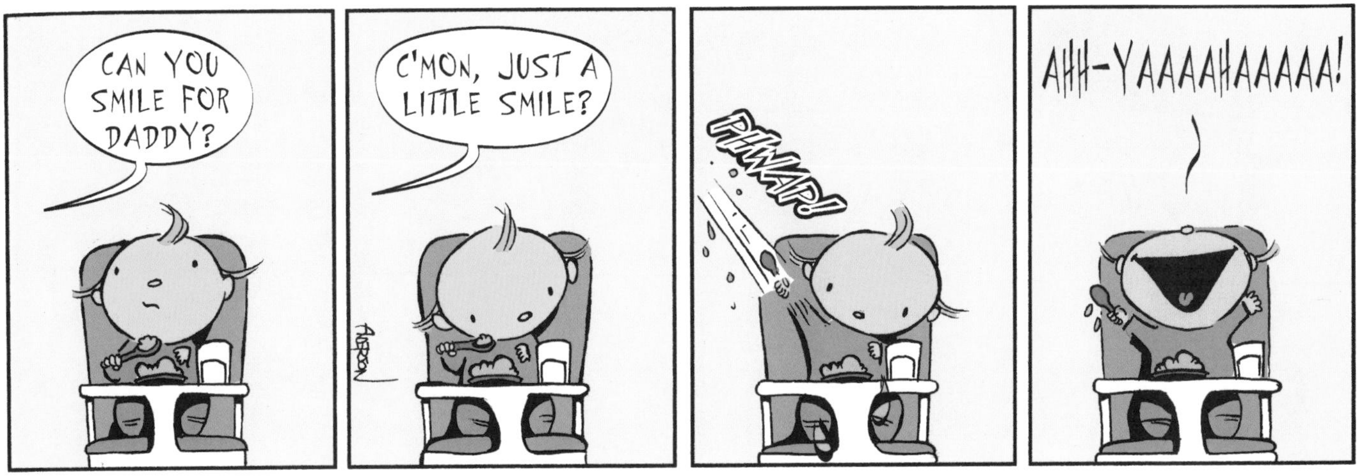
CAN YOU SMILE FOR DADDY?
C'MON, JUST A LITTLE SMILE?
PTHWAP!
AHH-YAAAAHAAAAA!

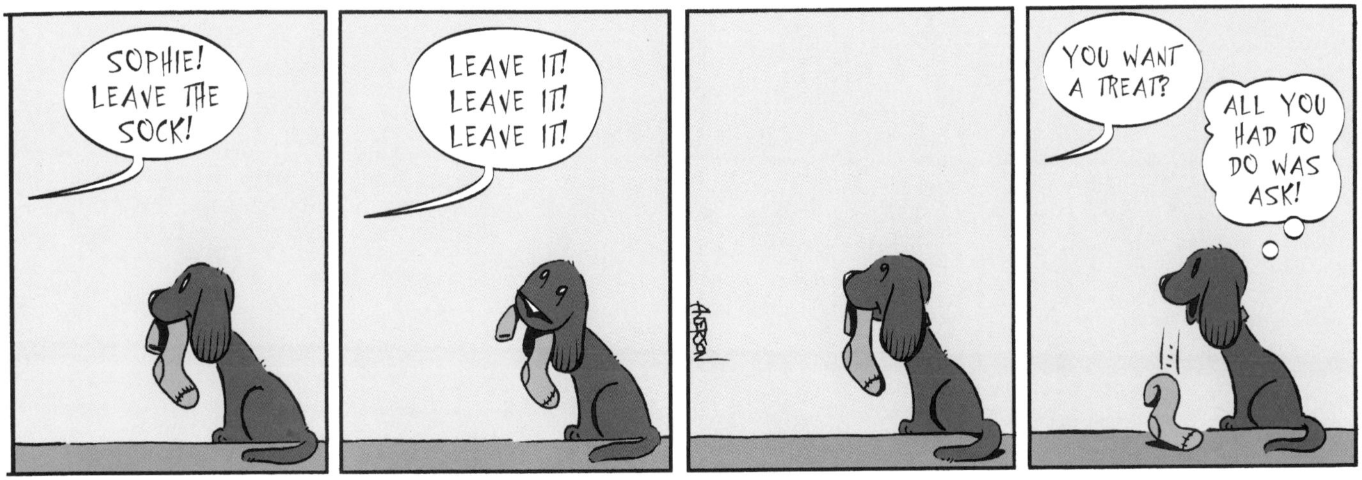
SOPHIE! LEAVE THE SOCK!
LEAVE IT! LEAVE IT! LEAVE IT!
YOU WANT A TREAT?
ALL YOU HAD TO DO WAS ASK!

SMILE, AND DON'T MOVE!
NEVERMIND!

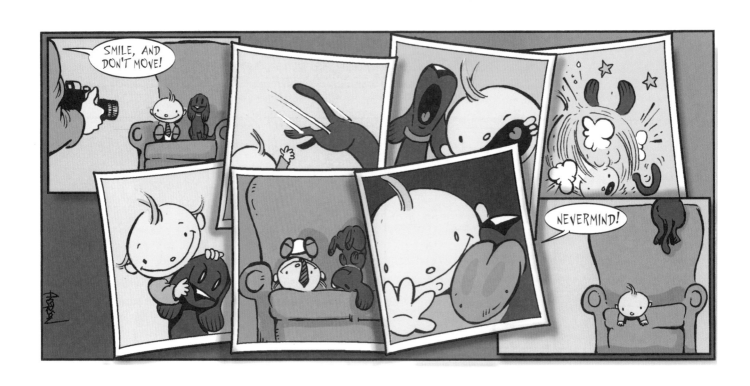

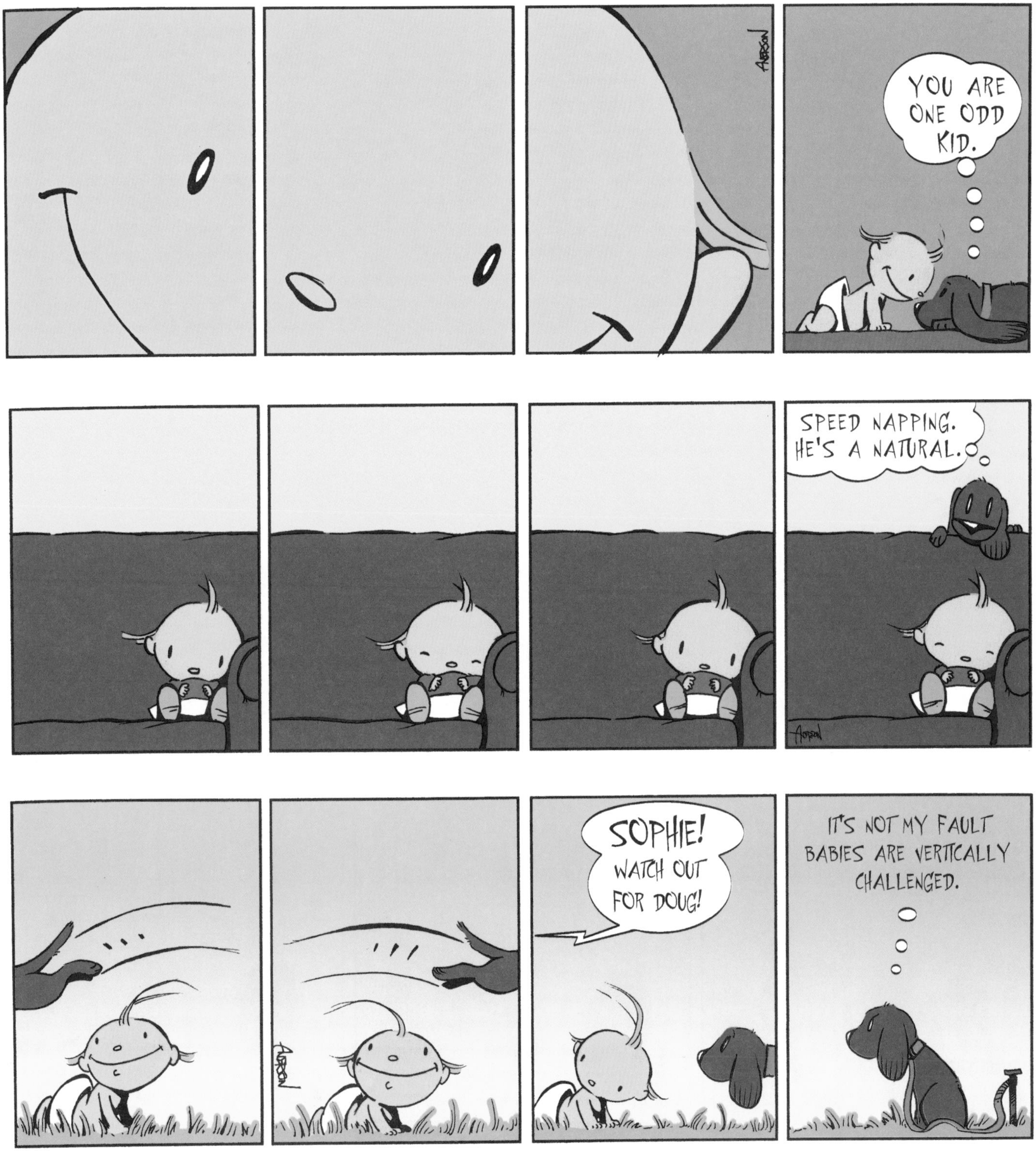
YOU ARE ONE ODD KID.
SPEED NAPPING. HE'S A NATURAL.
SOPHIE! WATCH OUT FOR DOUG!
IT'S NOT MY FAULT BABIES ARE VERTICALLY CHALLENGED.

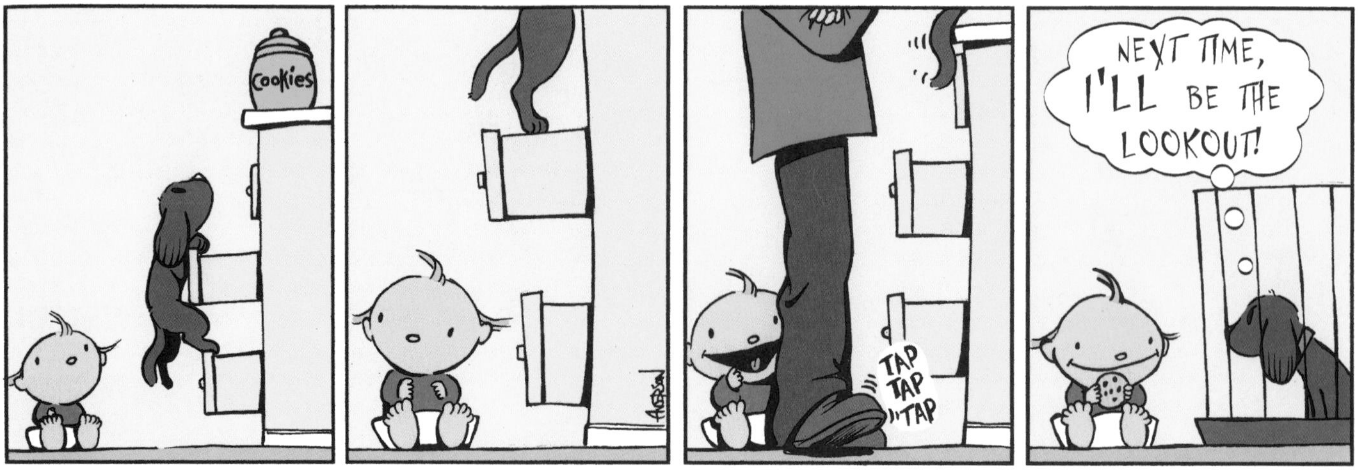
Cookies
TAP TAP TAP
NEXT TIME, I'LL BE THE LOOKOUT!

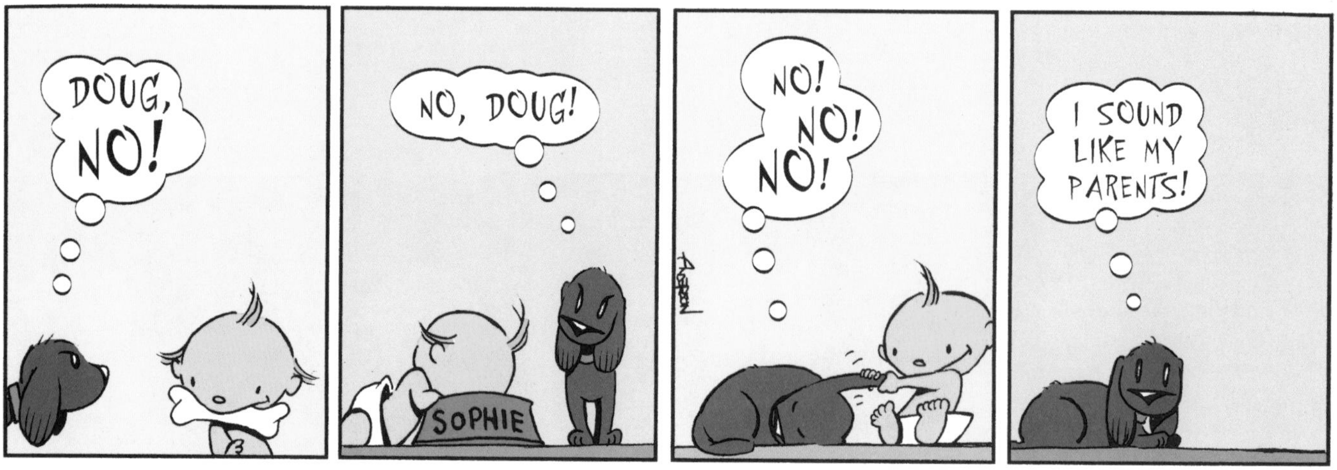
DOUG, NO!
NO, DOUG!
SOPHIE
NO! NO! NO!
I SOUND LIKE MY PARENTS!

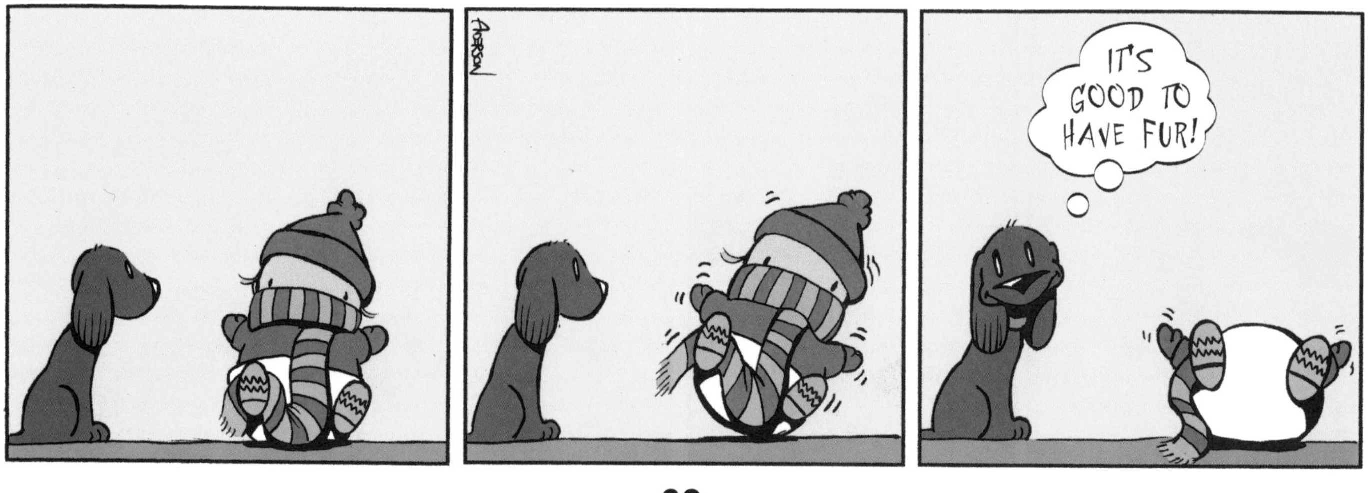
IT'S GOOD TO HAVE FUR!

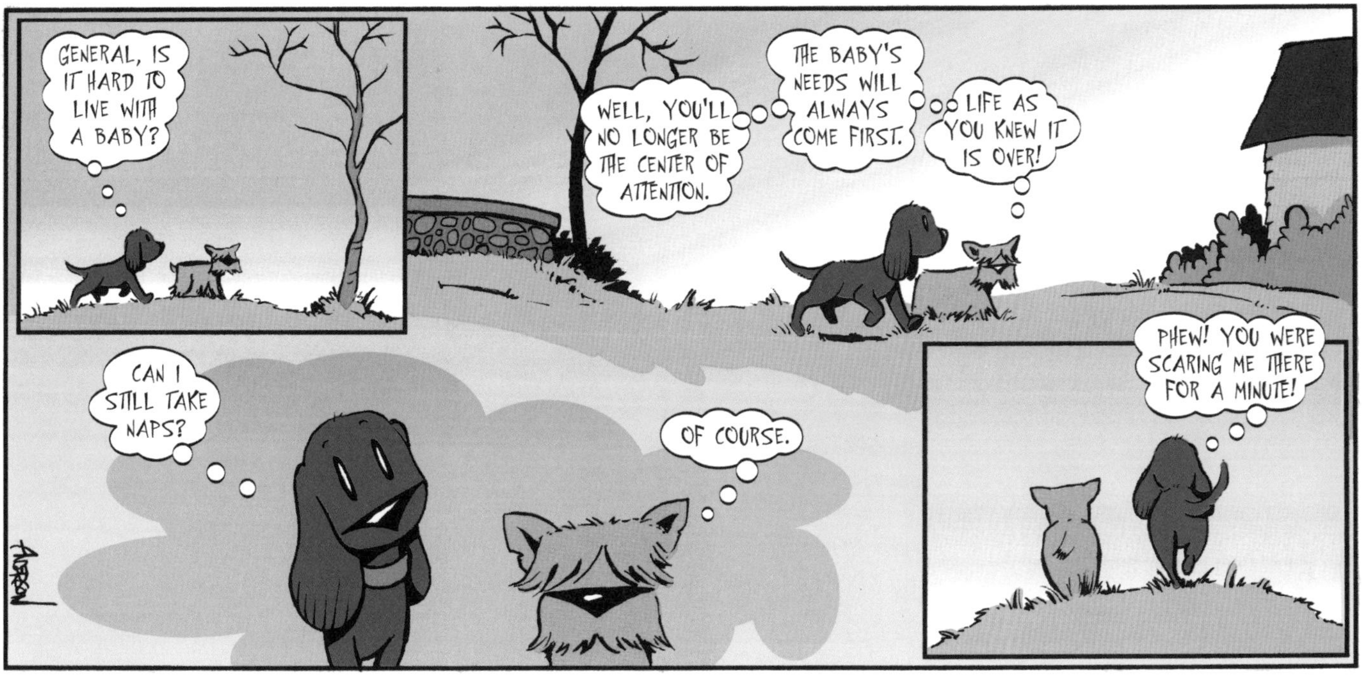
GENERAL, IS IT HARD TO LIVE WITH A BABY?
WELL, YOU'LL NO LONGER BE THE CENTER OF ATTENTION.
THE BABY'S NEEDS WILL ALWAYS COME FIRST.
LIFE AS YOU KNEW IT IS OVER!
CAN I STILL TAKE NAPS?
OF COURSE.
PHEW! YOU WERE SCARING ME THERE FOR A MINUTE!

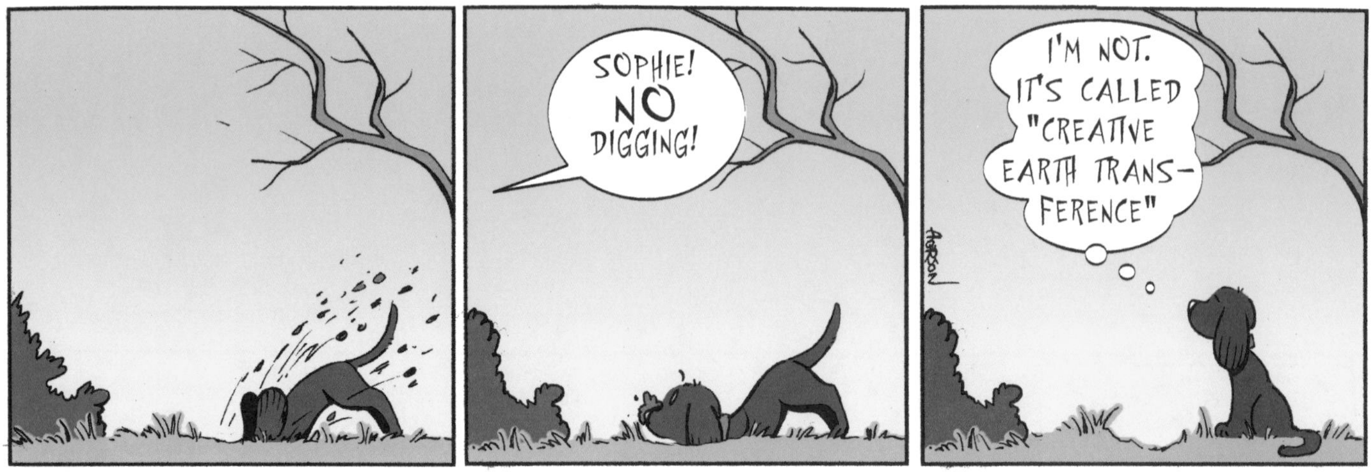
SOPHIE! NO DIGGING!
I'M NOT. IT'S CALLED "CREATIVE EARTH TRANS-FERENCE"

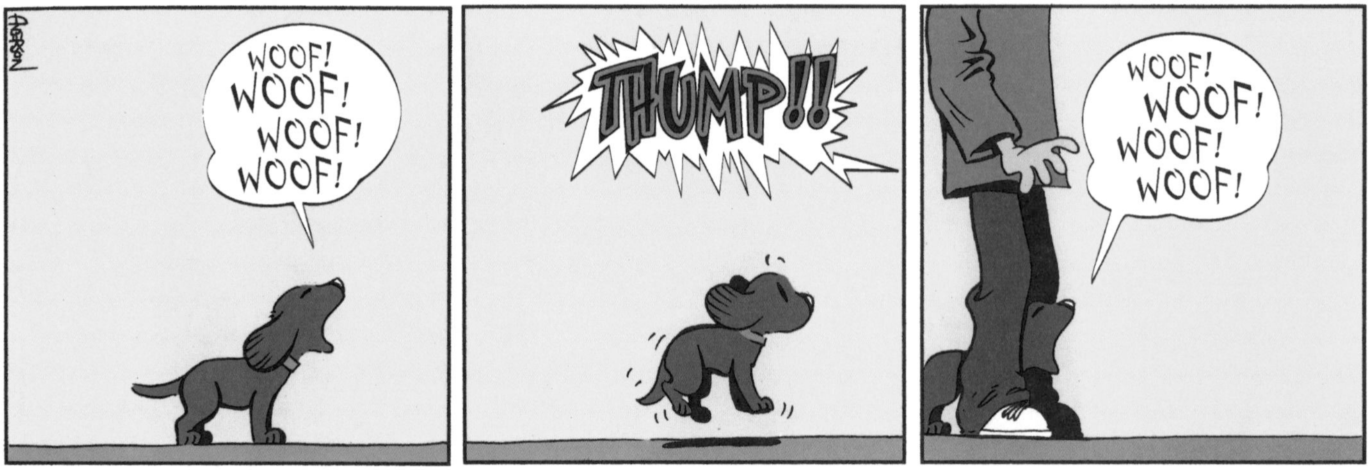
WOOF! WOOF! WOOF! WOOF!
THUMP!!
WOOF! WOOF! WOOF! WOOF!

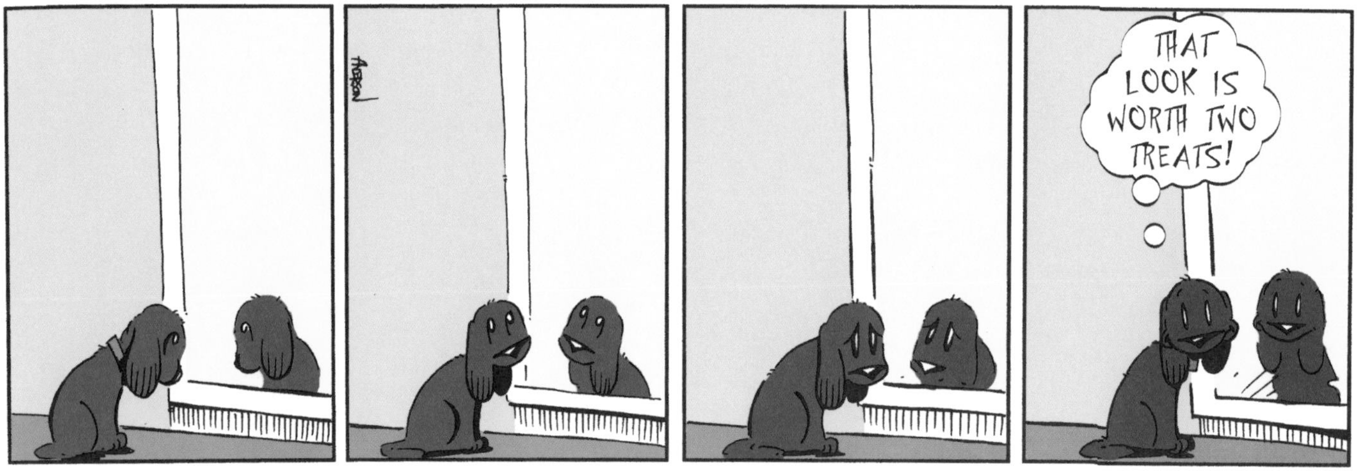
THAT LOOK IS WORTH TWO TREATS!

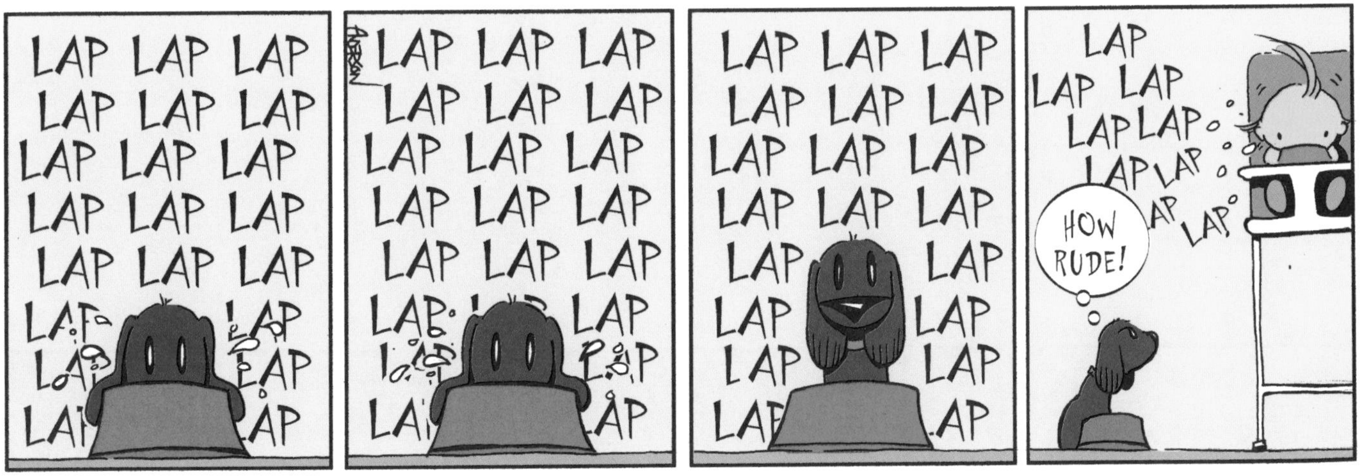
LAP LAP LAP
LAP LAP LAP
LAP LAP LAP
LAP LAP LAP
LAP LAP LAP
LAP LAP LAP
LAP LAP LAP
LAP LAP LAP
LAP LAP LAP
LAP LAP LAP
LAP LAP LAP
LAP LAP LAP
LAP LAP LAP
LAP LAP LAP
LAP LAP LAP
LAP LAP
LAP LAP
LAP LAP
LAP
LAP LAP
LAP LAP
LAP LAP
LAP LAP
HOW RUDE!

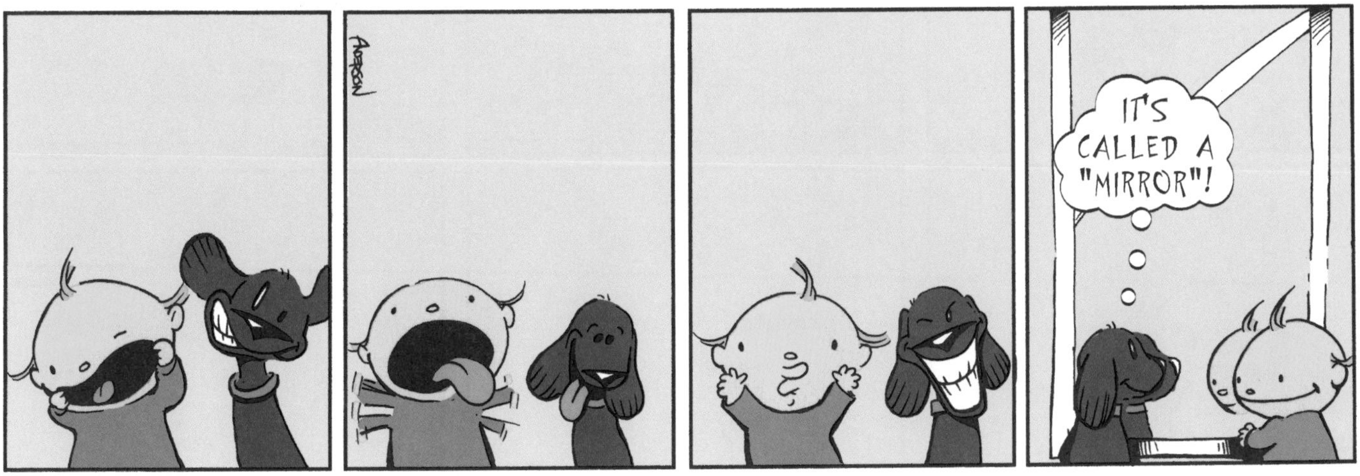
IT'S CALLED A "MIRROR"!

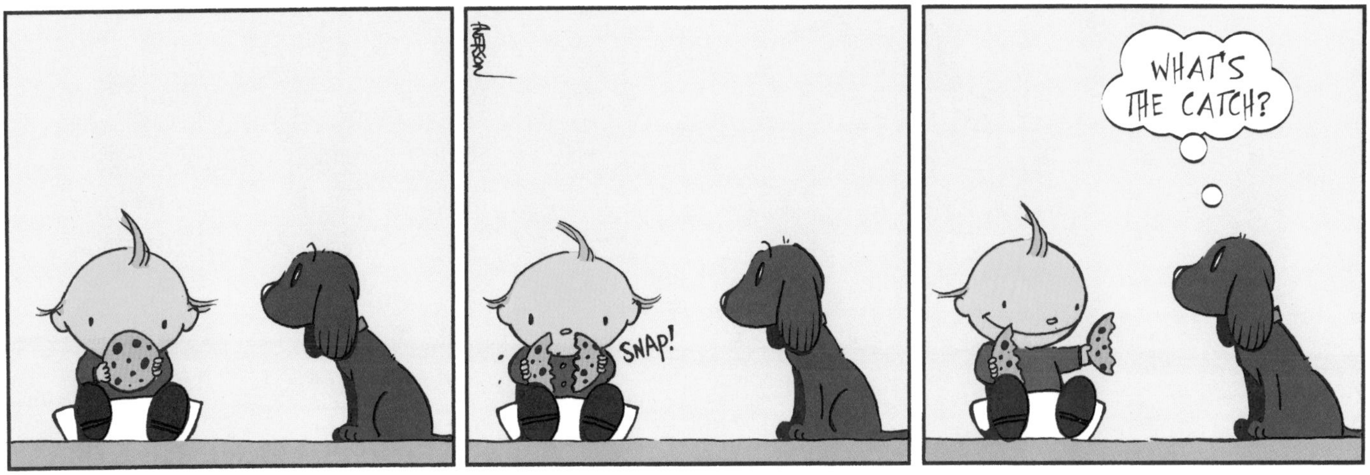
SNAP!
WHAT'S THE CATCH?

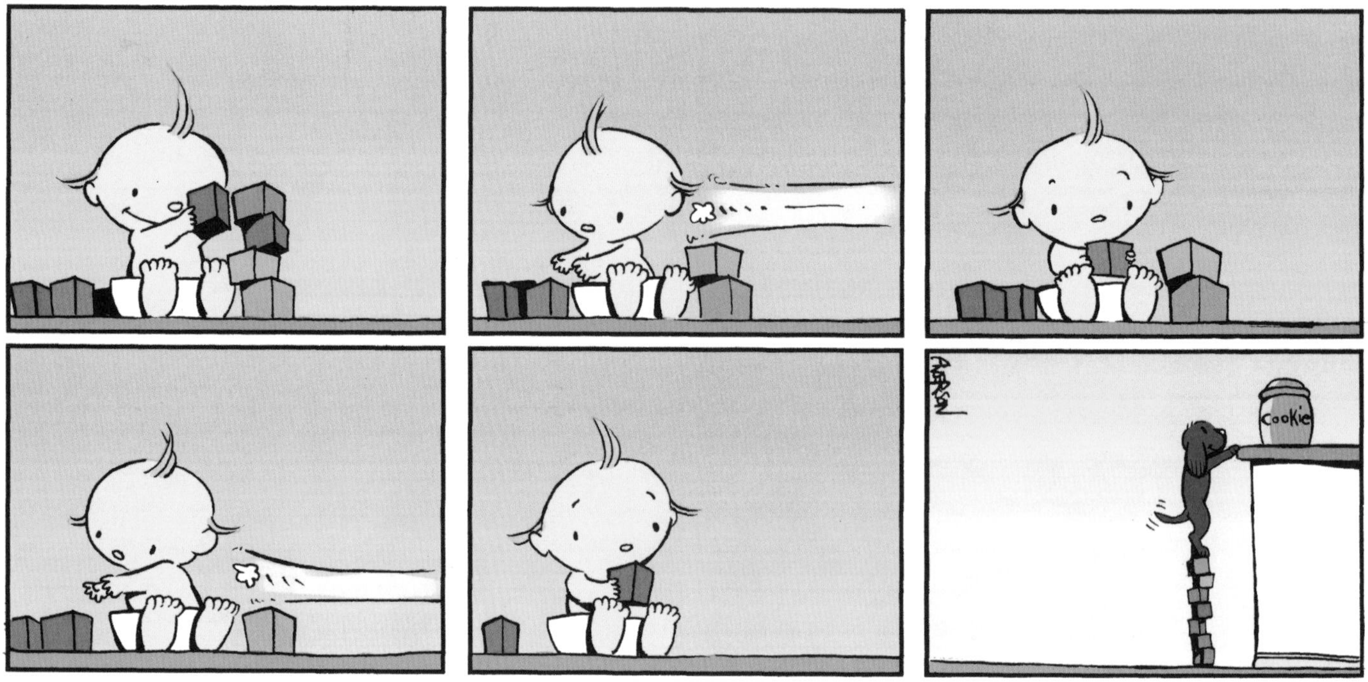
ANDERSON
Cookie

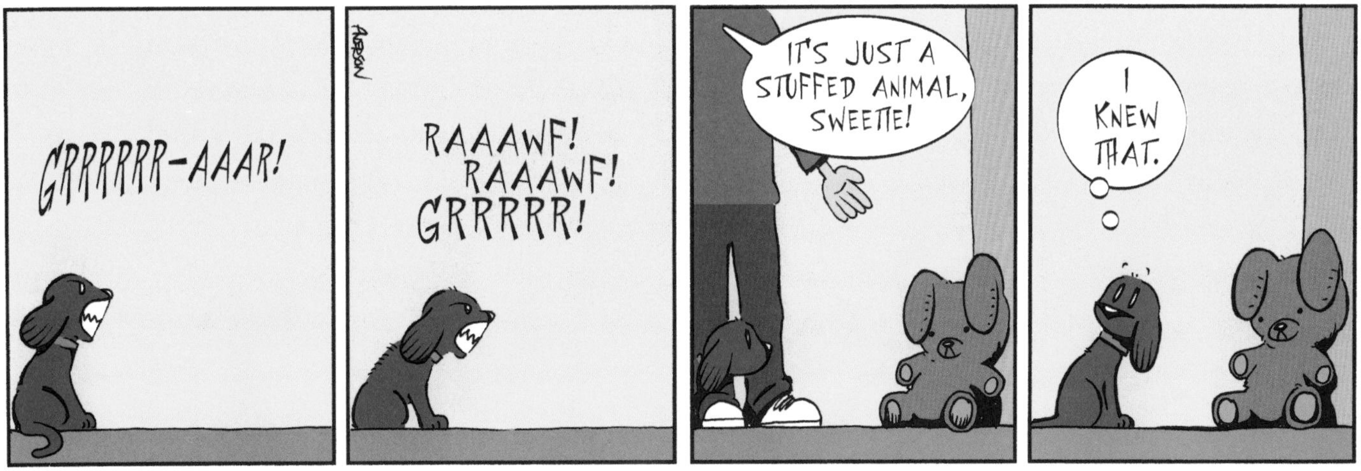
GRRRRRR-AAAR!
RAAAWF! RAAAWF! GRRRRR!
IT'S JUST A STUFFED ANIMAL, SWEETIE!
I KNEW THAT.

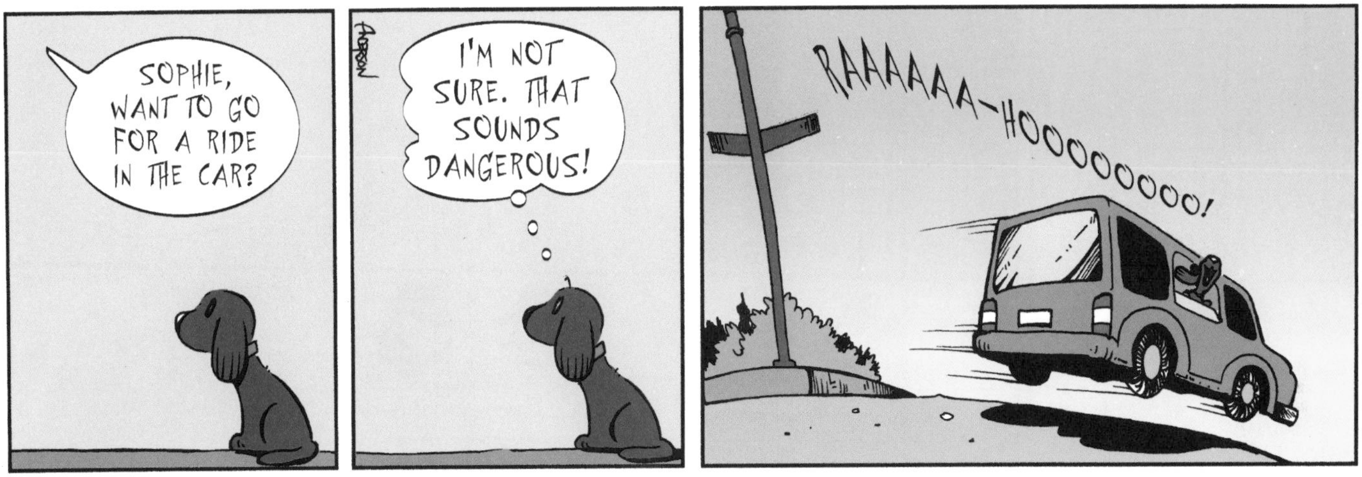
SOPHIE, WANT TO GO FOR A RIDE IN THE CAR?
I'M NOT SURE. THAT SOUNDS DANGEROUS!
RAAAAAA-HOOOOOOOOO!

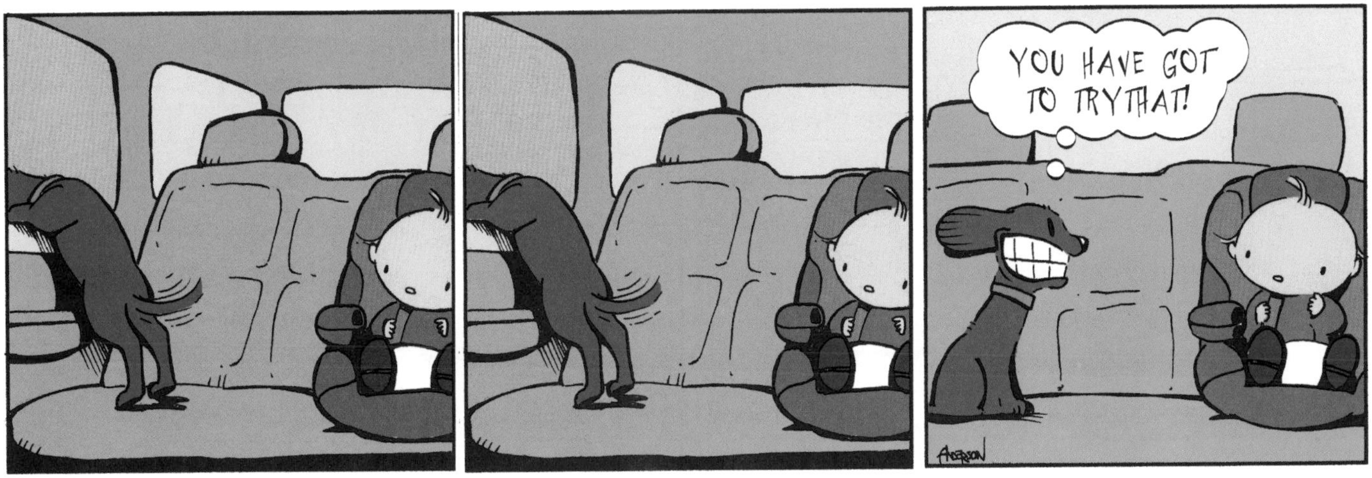
YOU HAVE GOT TO TRY THAT!

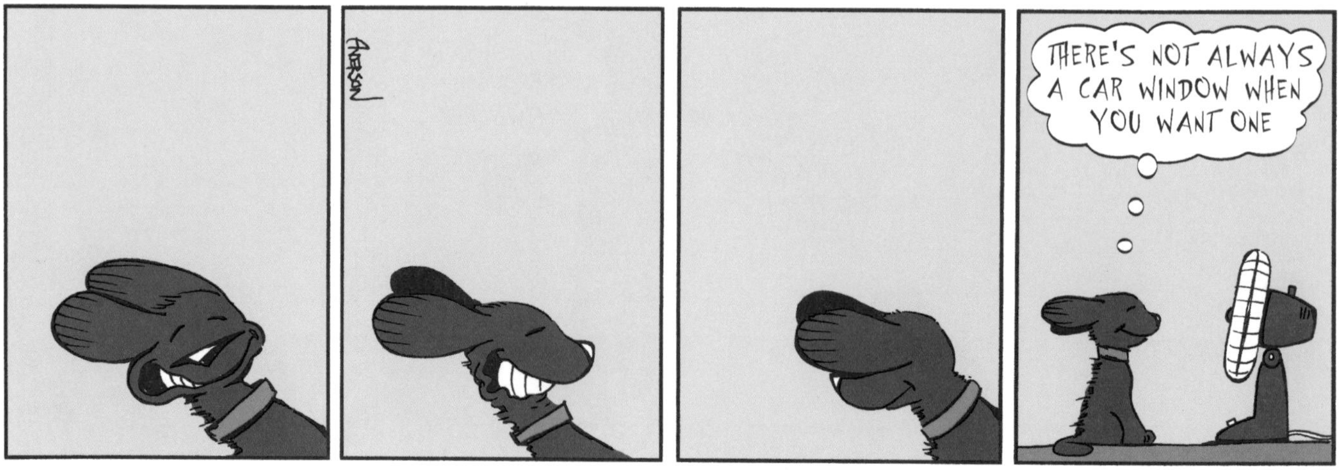
THERE'S NOT ALWAYS A CAR WINDOW WHEN YOU WANT ONE

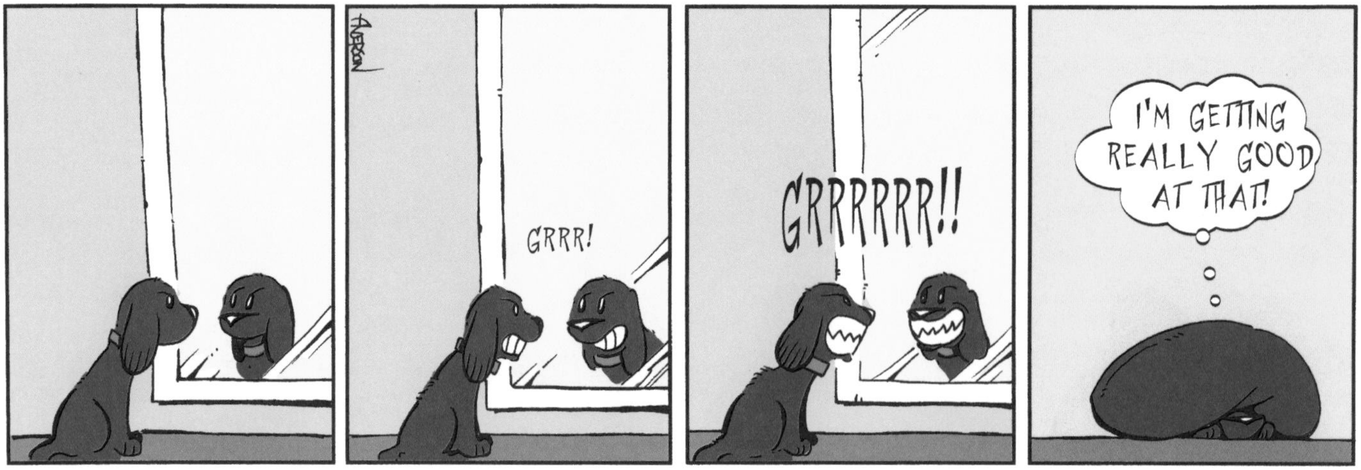
GRRR!
GRRRRRR!!
I'M GETTING REALLY GOOD AT THAT!

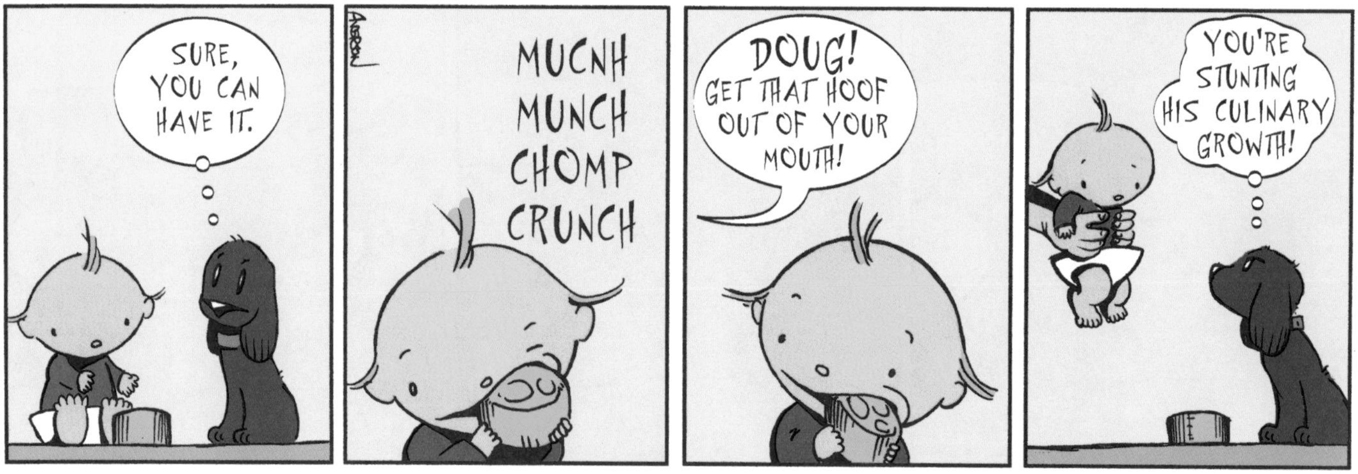
SURE, YOU CAN HAVE IT.
MUCNH
MUNCH
CHOMP
CRUNCH
DOUG! GET THAT HOOF OUT OF YOUR MOUTH!
YOU'RE STUNTING HIS CULINARY GROWTH!

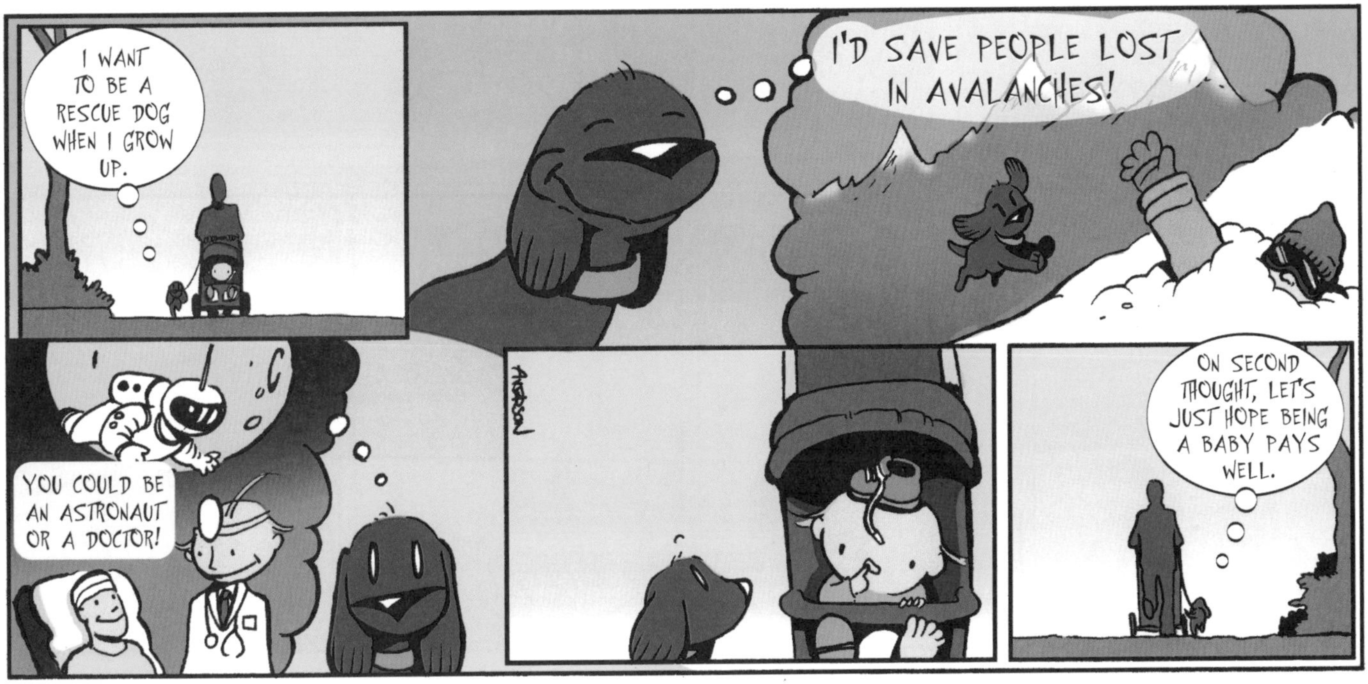
I WANT TO BE A RESCUE DOG WHEN I GROW UP.
I'D SAVE PEOPLE LOST IN AVALANCHES!
YOU COULD BE AN ASTRONAUT OR A DOCTOR!
ANDERSON
ON SECOND THOUGHT, LET'S JUST HOPE BEING A BABY PAYS WELL.

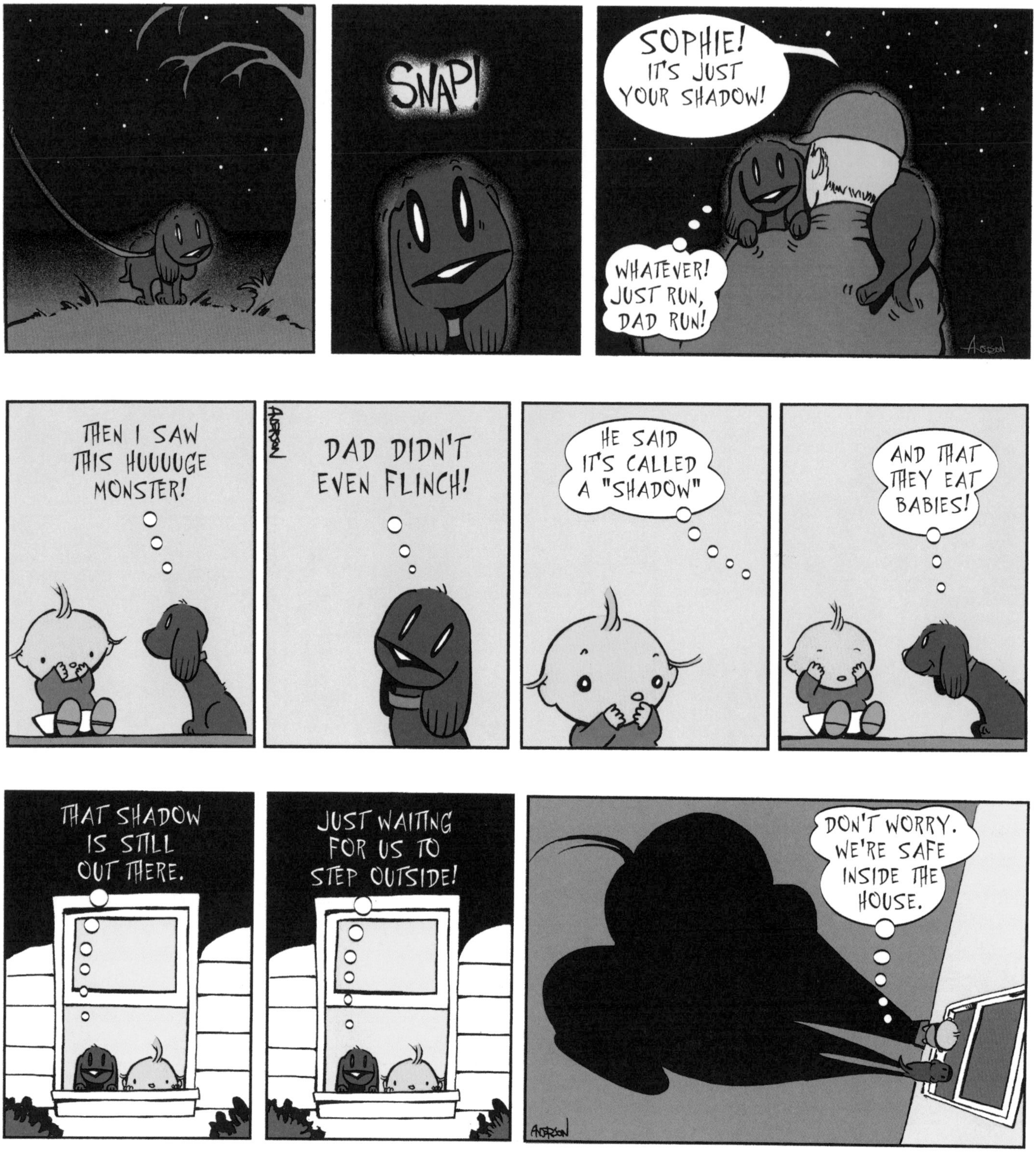
SNAP!
SOPHIE! IT'S JUST YOUR SHADOW!
WHATEVER! JUST RUN, DAD RUN!
ANDERSON
THEN I SAW THIS HUUUUGE MONSTER!
ANDERSON
DAD DIDN'T EVEN FLINCH!
HE SAID IT'S CALLED A "SHADOW"
AND THAT THEY EAT BABIES!
THAT SHADOW IS STILL OUT THERE.
JUST WAITING FOR US TO STEP OUTSIDE!
DON'T WORRY. WE'RE SAFE INSIDE THE HOUSE.
ANDERSON

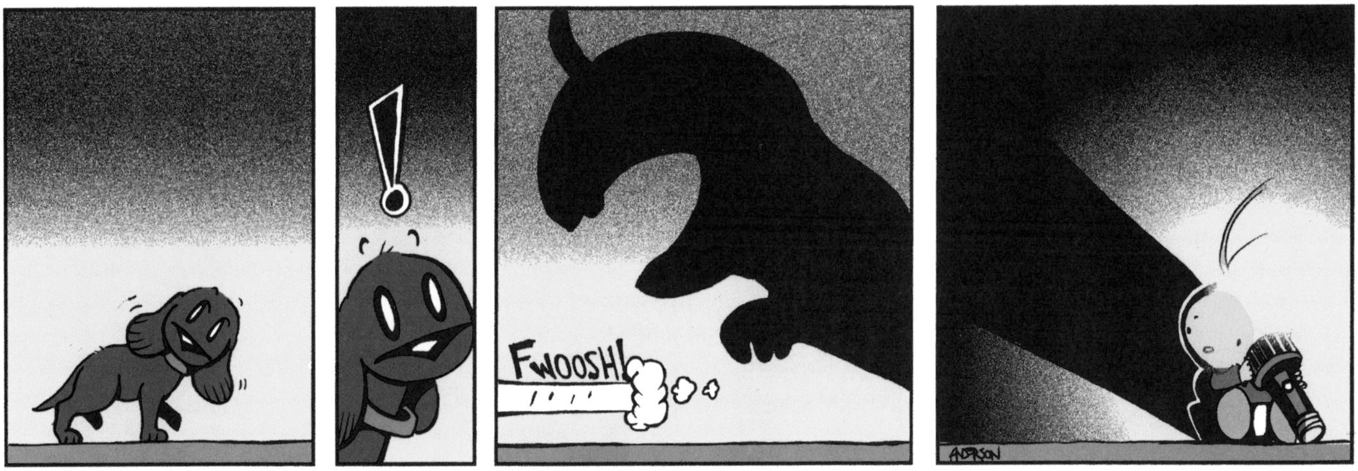
FWOOSH!

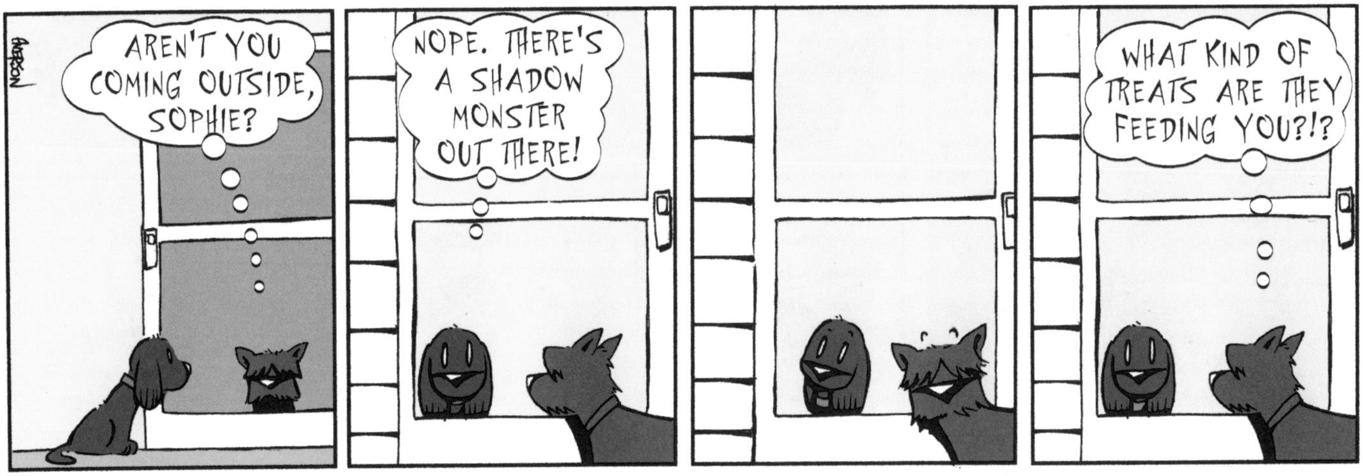
AREN'T YOU COMING OUTSIDE, SOPHIE?
NOPE. THERE'S A SHADOW MONSTER OUT THERE!
WHAT KIND OF TREATS ARE THEY FEEDING YOU?!?

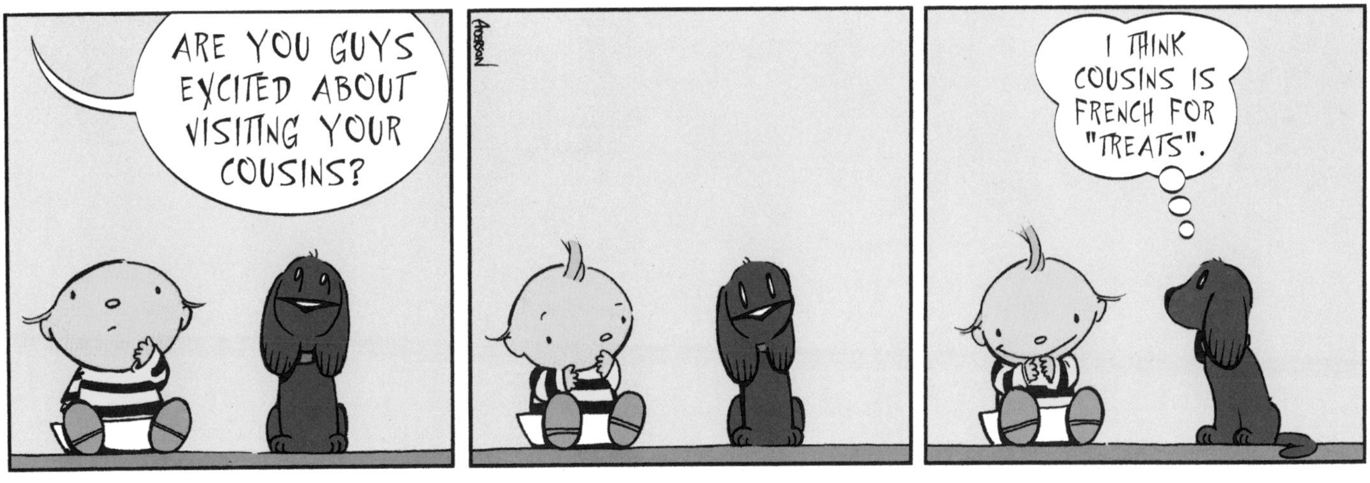
ARE YOU GUYS EXCITED ABOUT VISITING YOUR COUSINS?
I THINK COUSINS IS FRENCH FOR "TREATS".

LOOK WHAT MOMMY GOT YOU, DOUGIE!
HA! HA! HA! HA! HA! HA! HA!
WOW. THAT'S A GREAT LOOK...FOR A SEA URCHIN!
YOU LOOK LIKE A CLOWN WITH NO SENSE OF FASHION!
MOMMY DIDN'T FORGET YOU, SOPHIE!
THE IRONY IS BITING, ISN'T IT?
ANDERSON

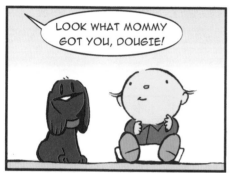

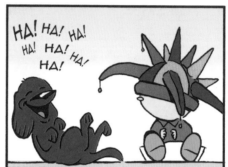

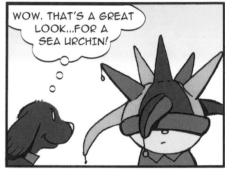

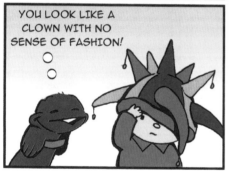

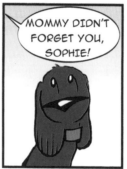

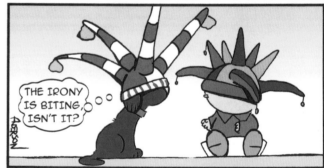

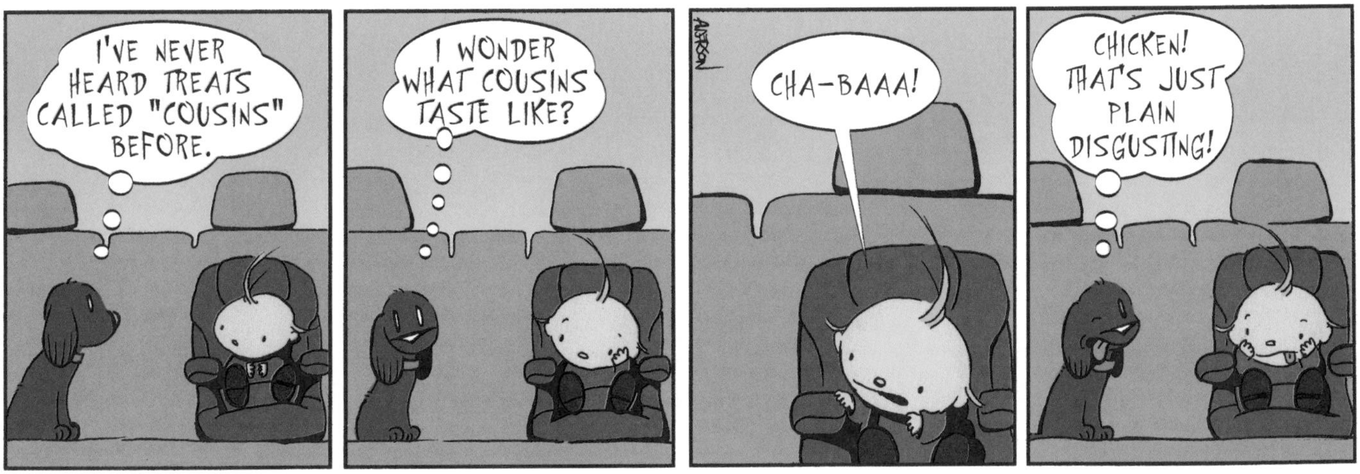
I'VE NEVER HEARD TREATS CALLED "COUSINS" BEFORE.
I WONDER WHAT COUSINS TASTE LIKE?
CHA-BAAA!
CHICKEN! THAT'S JUST PLAIN DISGUSTING!

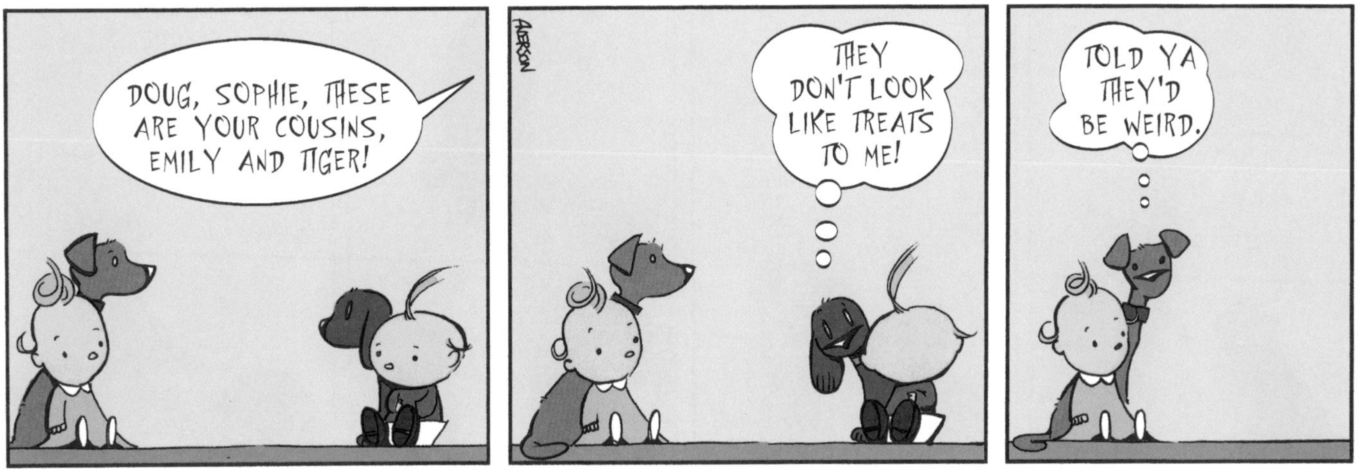
DOUG, SOPHIE, THESE ARE YOUR COUSINS, EMILY AND TIGER!
THEY DON'T LOOK LIKE TREATS TO ME!
TOLD YA THEY'D BE WEIRD.

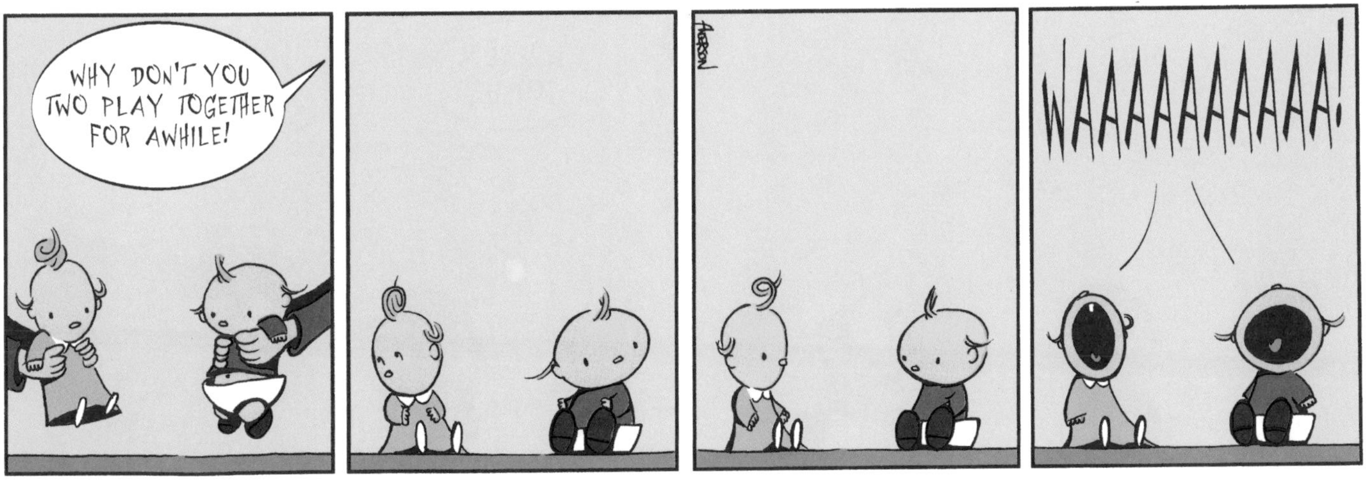
WHY DON'T YOU TWO PLAY TOGETHER FOR AWHILE!
WAAAAAAAAA!

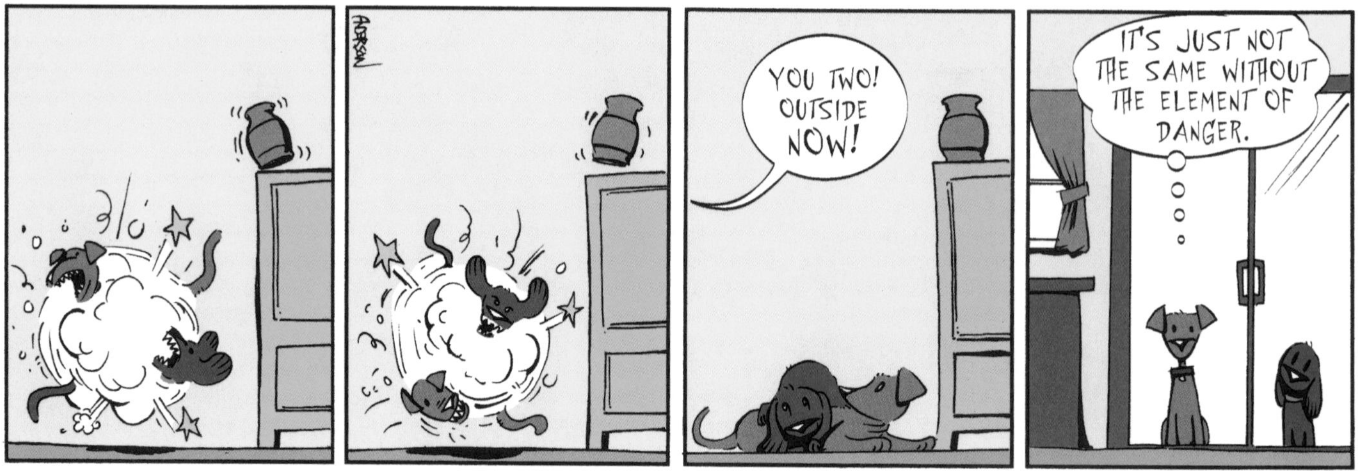
YOU TWO! OUTSIDE NOW!
IT'S JUST NOT THE SAME WITHOUT THE ELEMENT OF DANGER.

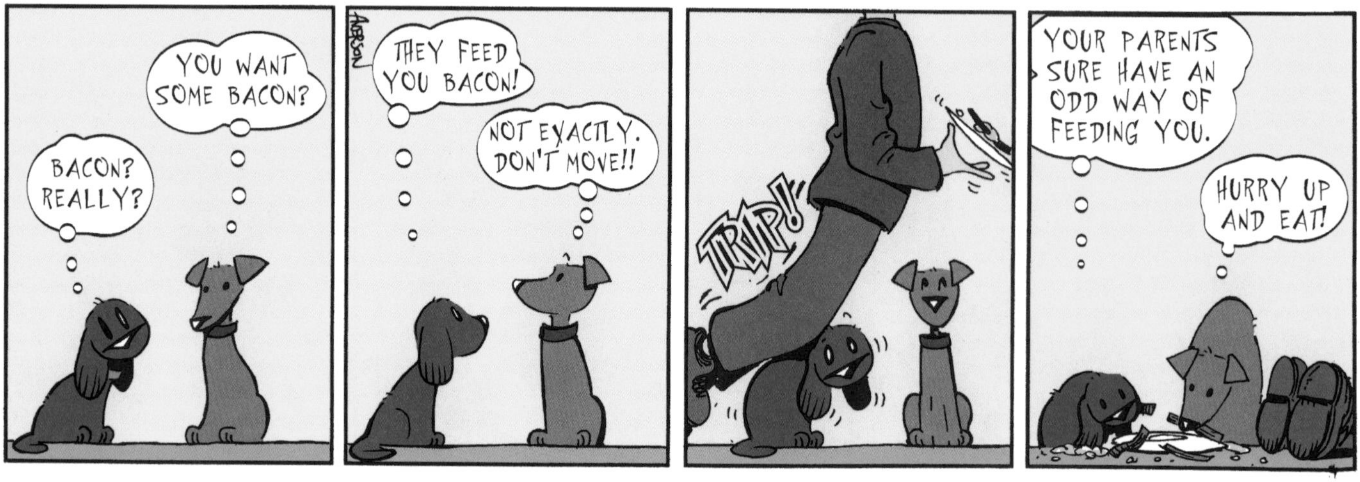
YOU WANT SOME BACON?
BACON? REALLY?
THEY FEED YOU BACON!
NOT EXACTLY. DON'T MOVE!!
TRIP!
YOUR PARENTS SURE HAVE AN ODD WAY OF FEEDING YOU.
HURRY UP AND EAT!

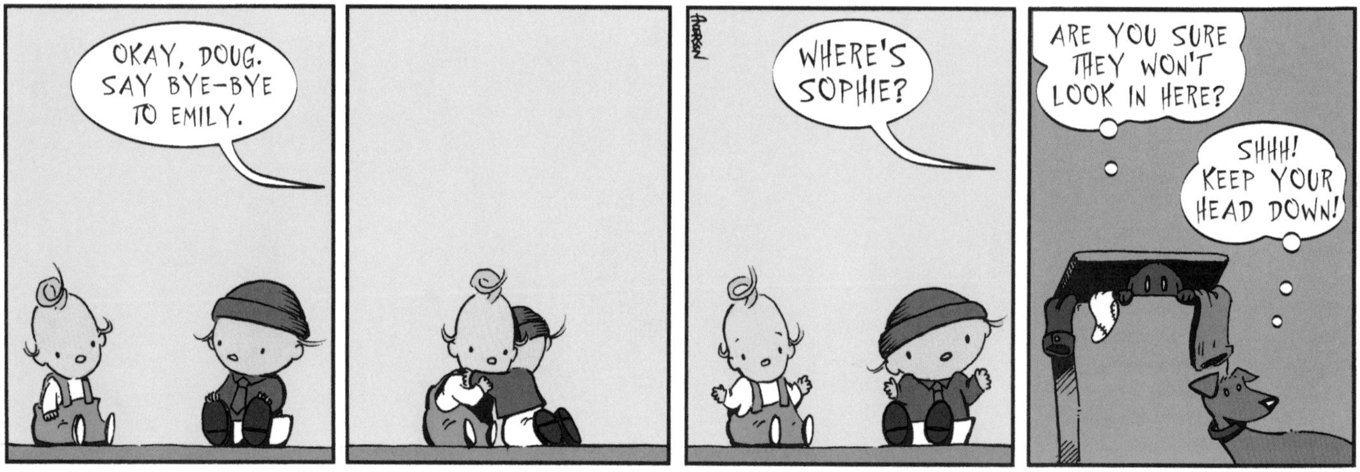
OKAY, DOUG. SAY BYE-BYE TO EMILY.
WHERE'S SOPHIE?
ARE YOU SURE THEY WON'T LOOK IN HERE?
SHHH! KEEP YOUR HEAD DOWN!

I'VE FIGURED YOU OUT, SHADOW!
YOU'RE ATTACHED TO ME!
AND YOU HAVE TO DO WHATEVER I WANT!
I'M NOT SCARED OF YOU ANYMORE!
SO-SO!
FWOOSH!
HONEY, DID YOU KNOW SOPHIE COULD CLIMB TREES?!?
ANDERSON

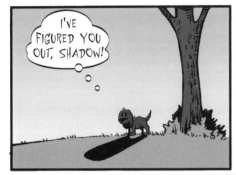

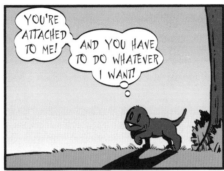

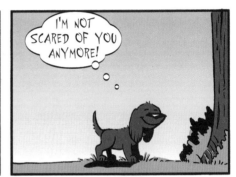

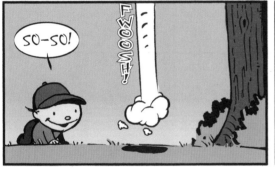

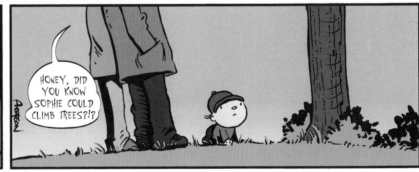

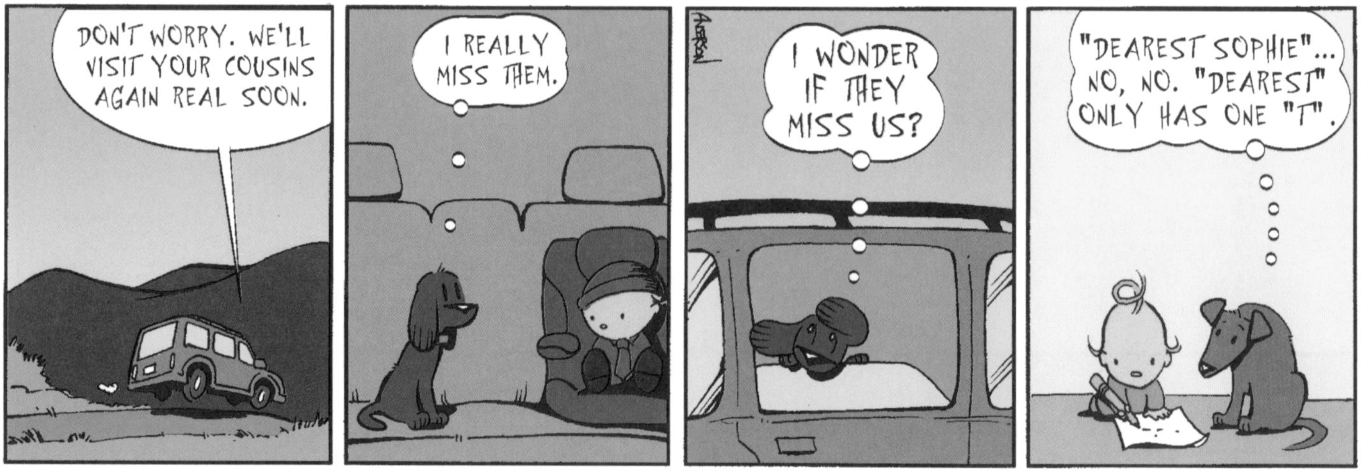
DON'T WORRY. WE'LL VISIT YOUR COUSINS AGAIN REAL SOON.
I REALLY MISS THEM.
I WONDER IF THEY MISS US?
"DEAREST SOPHIE"... NO, NO. "DEAREST" ONLY HAS ONE "T".

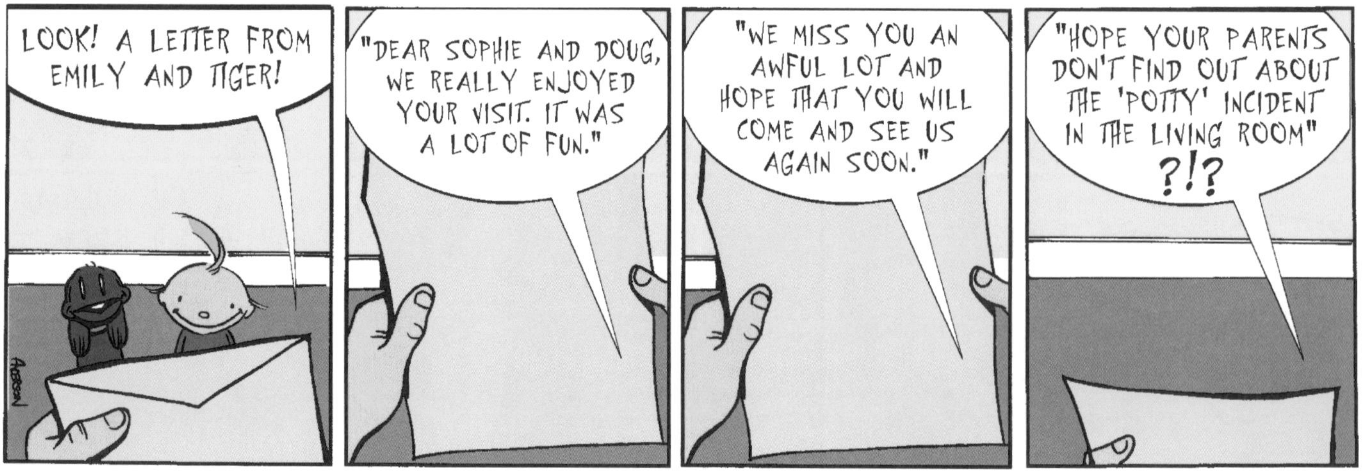
LOOK! A LETTER FROM EMILY AND TIGER!
"DEAR SOPHIE AND DOUG, WE REALLY ENJOYED YOUR VISIT. IT WAS A LOT OF FUN."
"WE MISS YOU AN AWFUL LOT AND HOPE THAT YOU WILL COME AND SEE US AGAIN SOON."
"HOPE YOUR PARENTS DON'T FIND OUT ABOUT THE 'POTTY' INCIDENT IN THE LIVING ROOM"
?!?

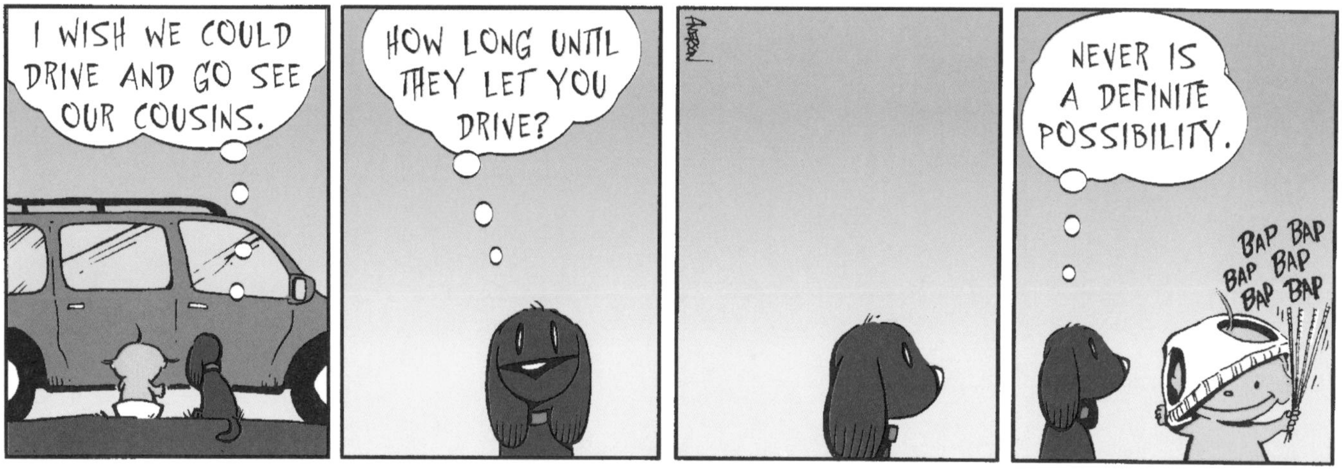
I WISH WE COULD DRIVE AND GO SEE OUR COUSINS.
HOW LONG UNTIL THEY LET YOU DRIVE?
NEVER IS A DEFINITE POSSIBILITY.
BAP BAP BAP BAP BAP BAP

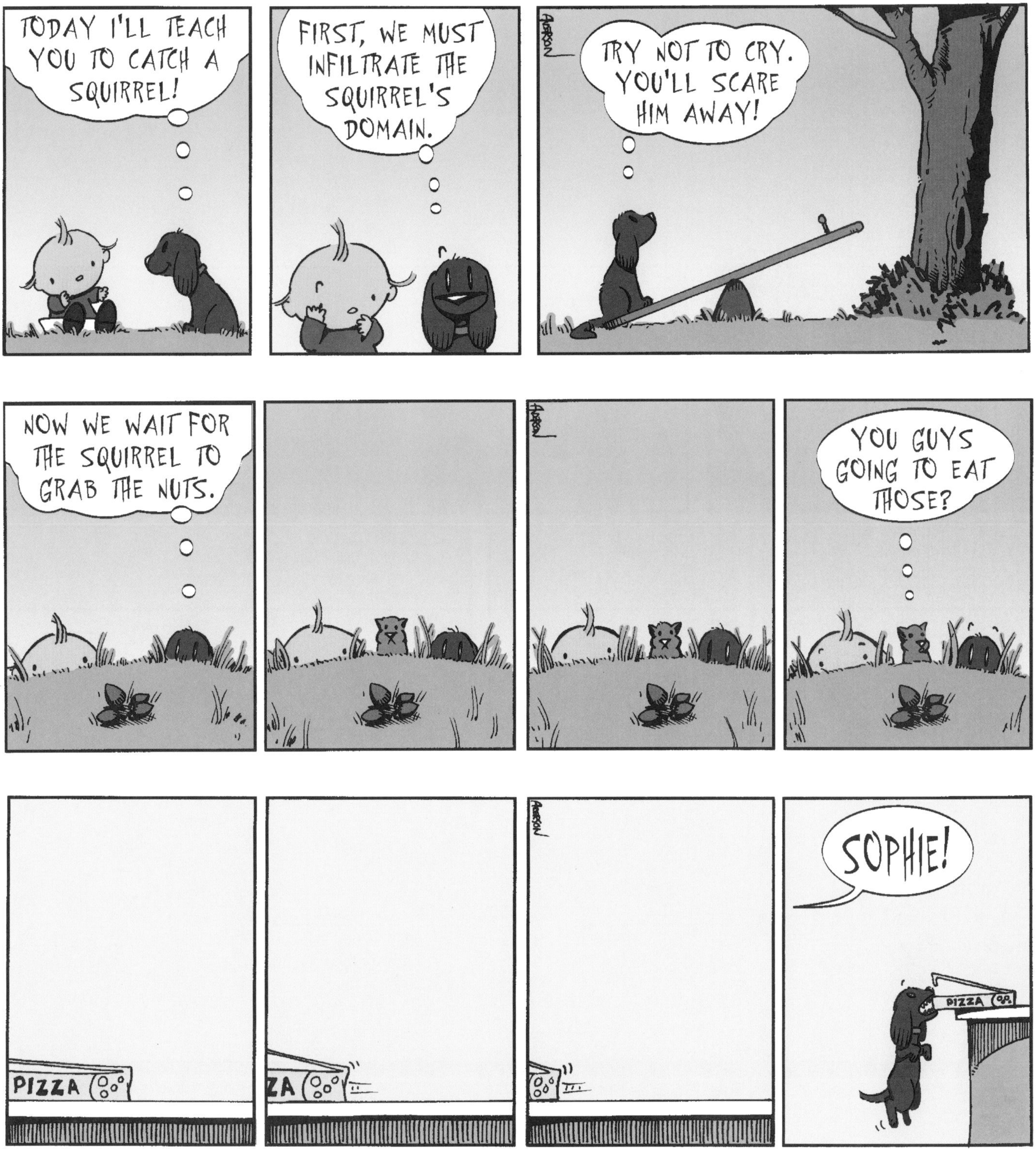
TODAY I'LL TEACH YOU TO CATCH A SQUIRREL!
FIRST, WE MUST INFILTRATE THE SQUIRREL'S DOMAIN.
TRY NOT TO CRY. YOU'LL SCARE HIM AWAY!
NOW WE WAIT FOR THE SQUIRREL TO GRAB THE NUTS.
YOU GUYS GOING TO EAT THOSE?
PIZZA
ZA
SOPHIE!
PIZZA

48

WHAT ARE YOU GUYS DOING?
CATCHING A SQUIRREL.
DO YOU KNOW WHAT SQUIRRELS LOOK LIKE?
DO YOU?
YAH. THERE'S ONE RIGHT OVER THERE!
THANKS! LET'S GO GET 'IM, DOUG!
GOOD LUCK!

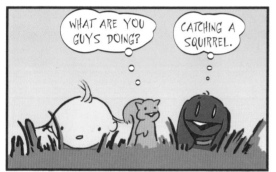

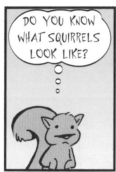

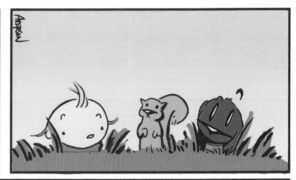

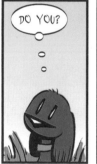

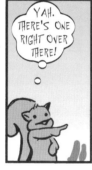

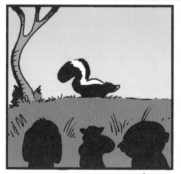

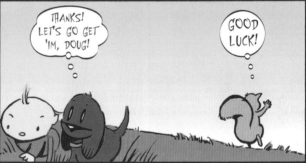

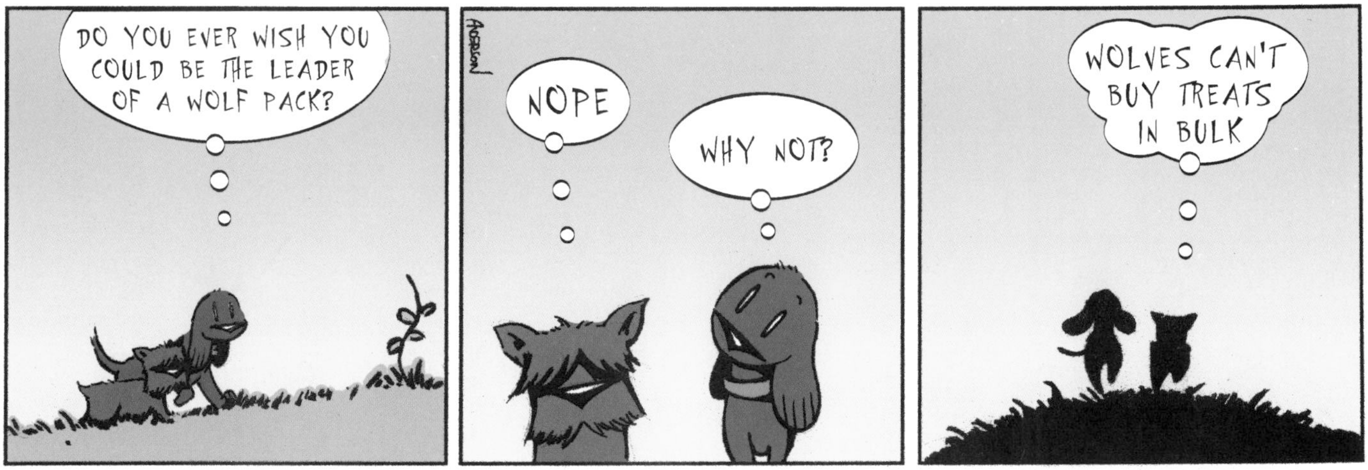
DO YOU EVER WISH YOU COULD BE THE LEADER OF A WOLF PACK?
NOPE
WHY NOT?
WOLVES CAN'T BUY TREATS IN BULK

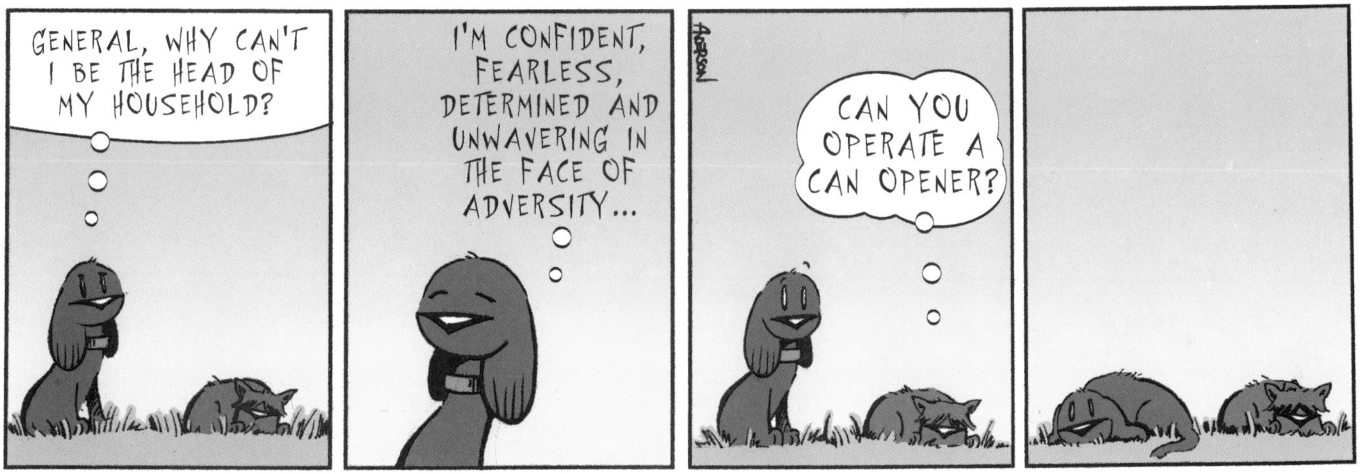
GENERAL, WHY CAN'T I BE THE HEAD OF MY HOUSEHOLD?
I'M CONFIDENT, FEARLESS, DETERMINED AND UNWAVERING IN THE FACE OF ADVERSITY...
CAN YOU OPERATE A CAN OPENER?

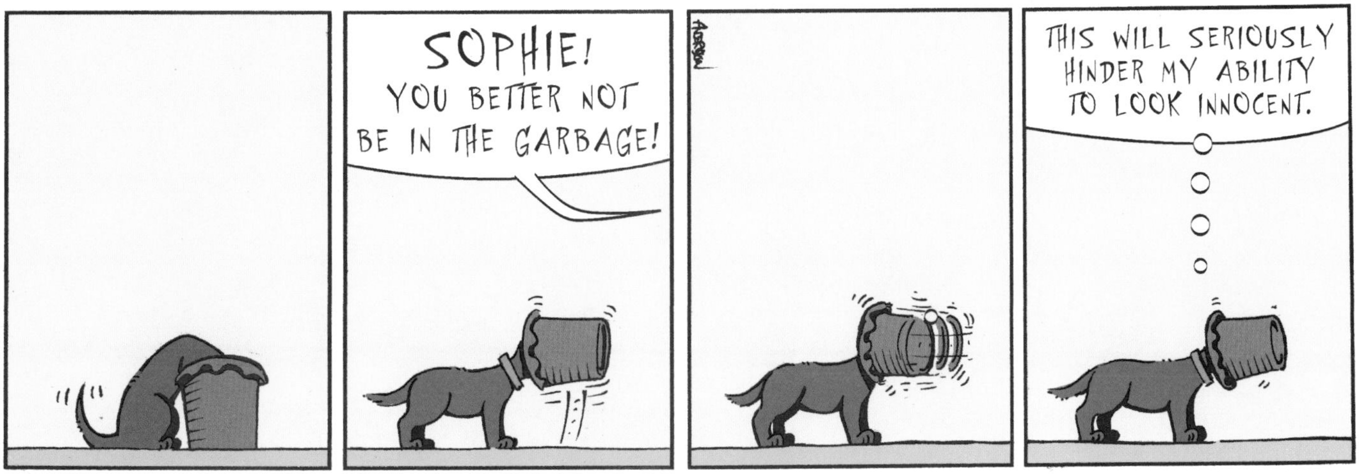
SOPHIE! YOU BETTER NOT BE IN THE GARBAGE!
THIS WILL SERIOUSLY HINDER MY ABILITY TO LOOK INNOCENT.

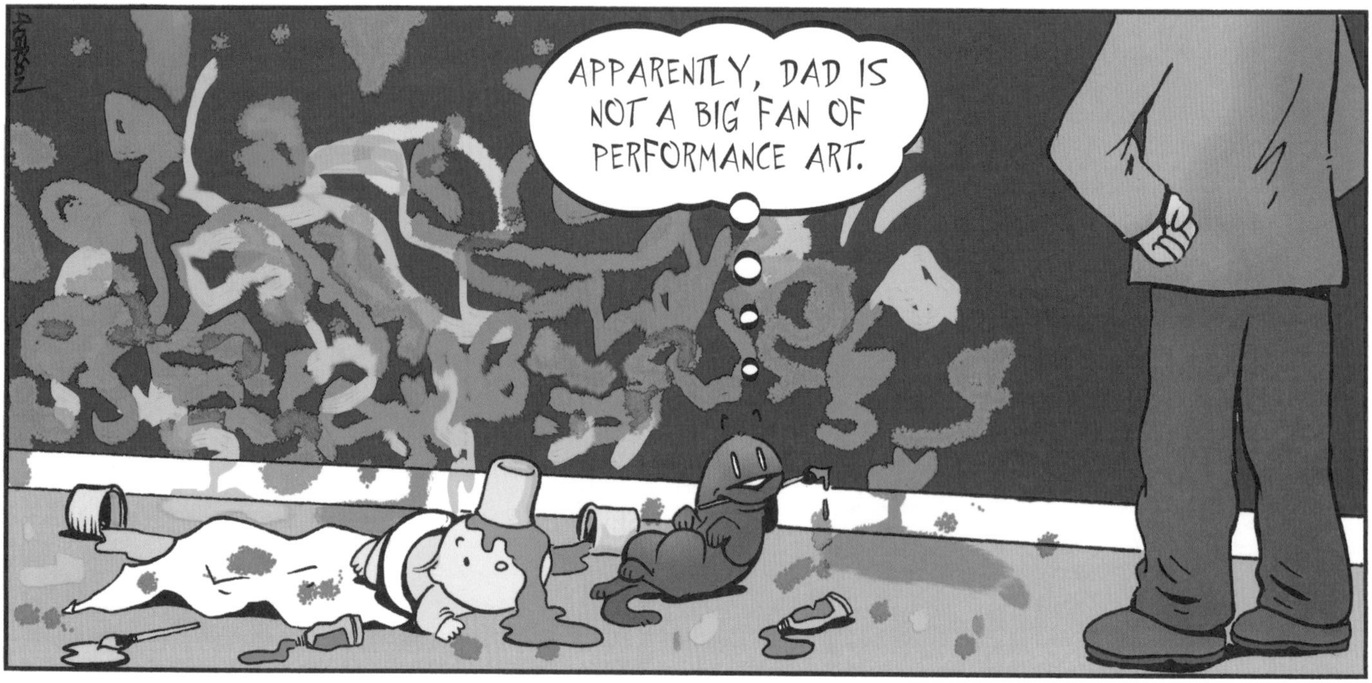
APPARENTLY, DAD IS NOT A BIG FAN OF PERFORMANCE ART.

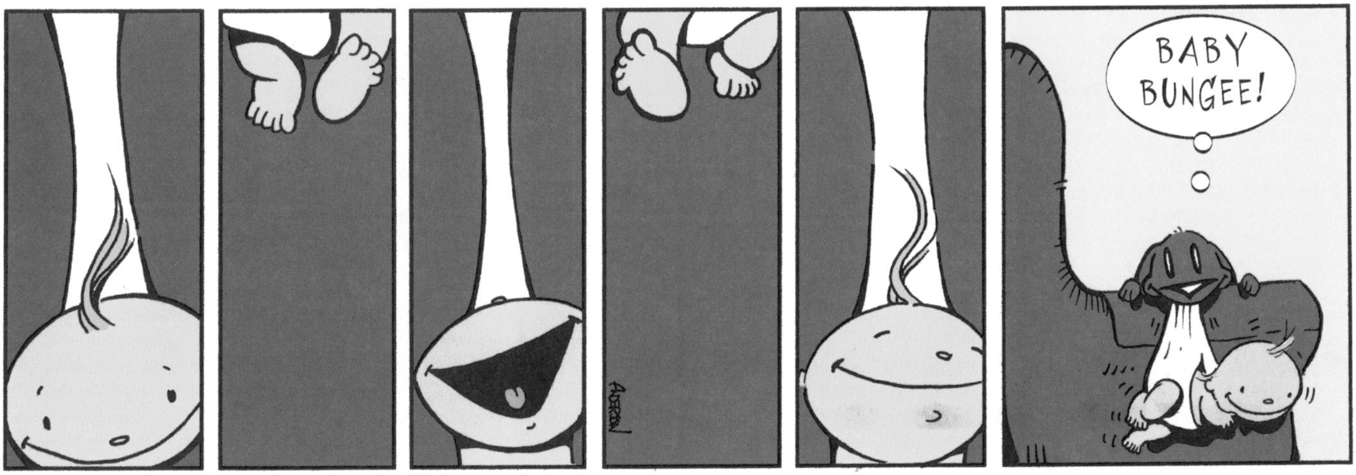
BABY BUNGEE!

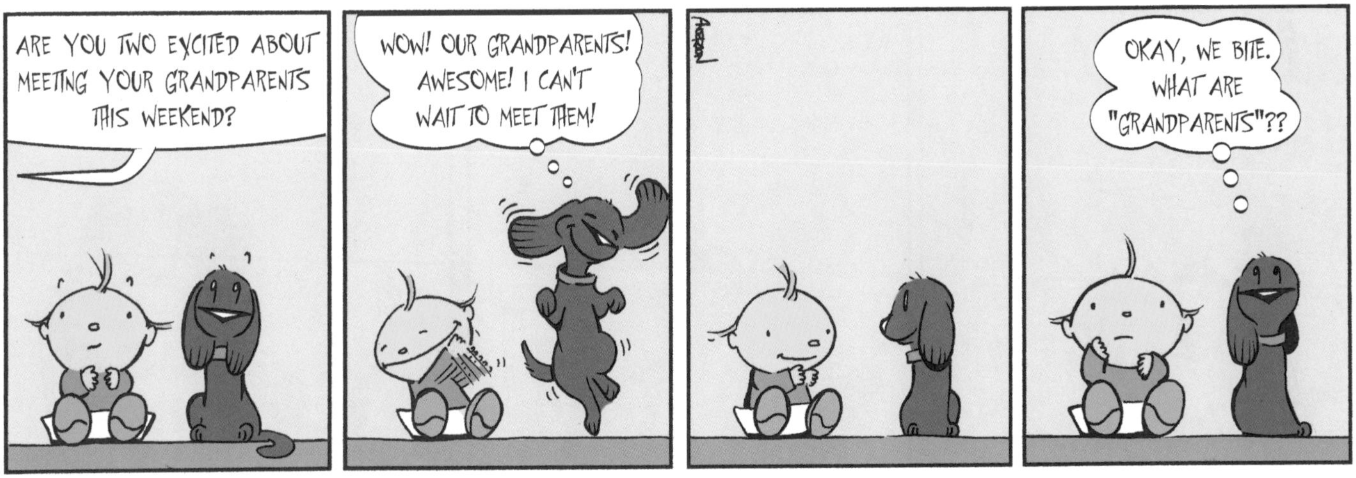
ARE YOU TWO EXCITED ABOUT MEETING YOUR GRANDPARENTS THIS WEEKEND?
WOW! OUR GRANDPARENTS! AWESOME! I CAN'T WAIT TO MEET THEM!
OKAY, WE BITE. WHAT ARE "GRANDPARENTS"??

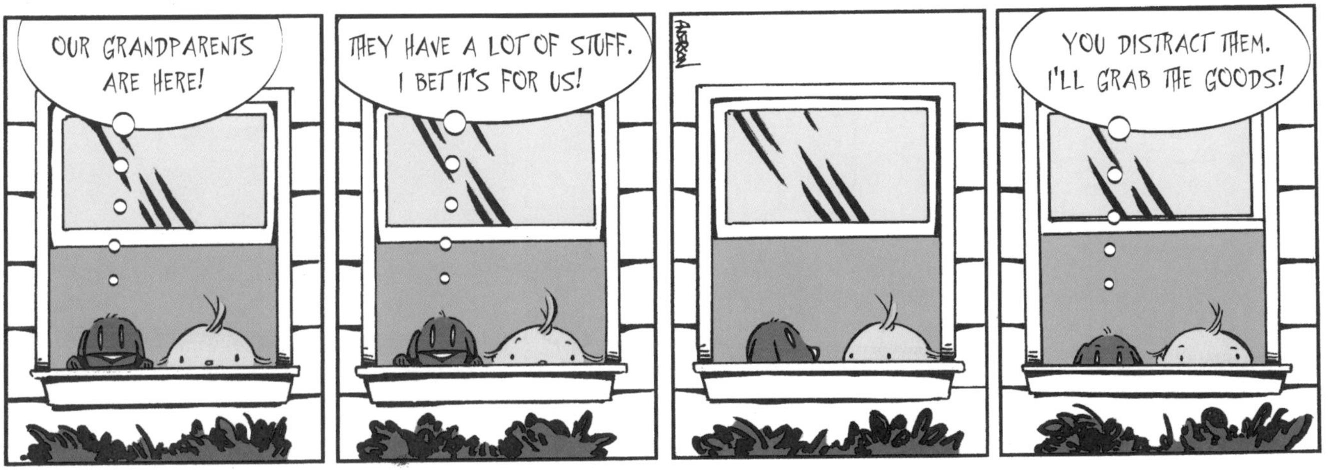
OUR GRANDPARENTS ARE HERE!
THEY HAVE A LOT OF STUFF. I BET IT'S FOR US!
YOU DISTRACT THEM. I'LL GRAB THE GOODS!

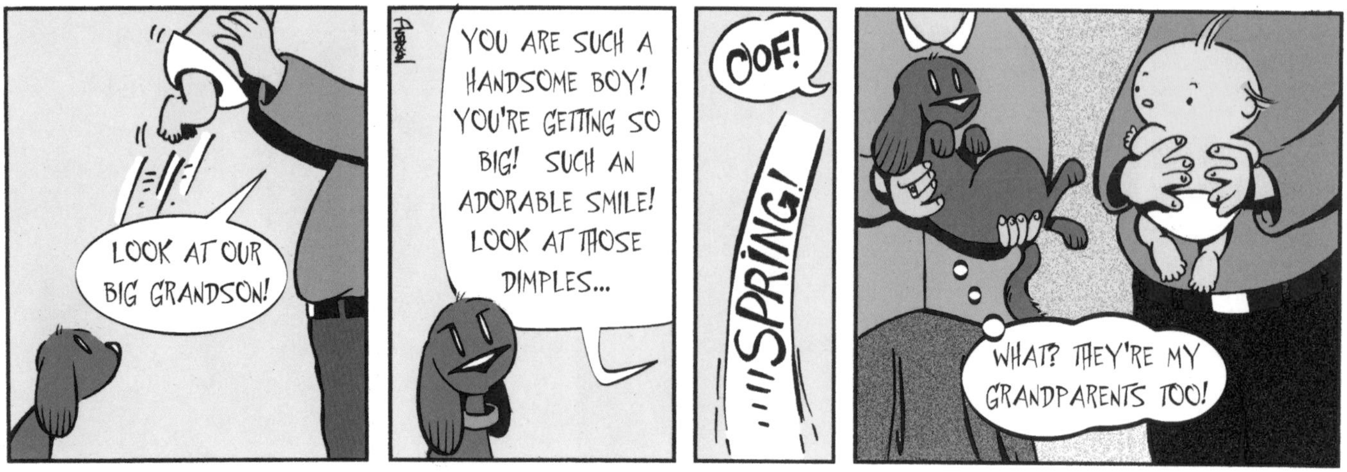
LOOK AT OUR BIG GRANDSON!
YOU ARE SUCH A HANDSOME BOY! YOU'RE GETTING SO BIG! SUCH AN ADORABLE SMILE! LOOK AT THOSE DIMPLES...
OOF!
SPRiNG!
WHAT? THEY'RE MY GRANDPARENTS TOO!

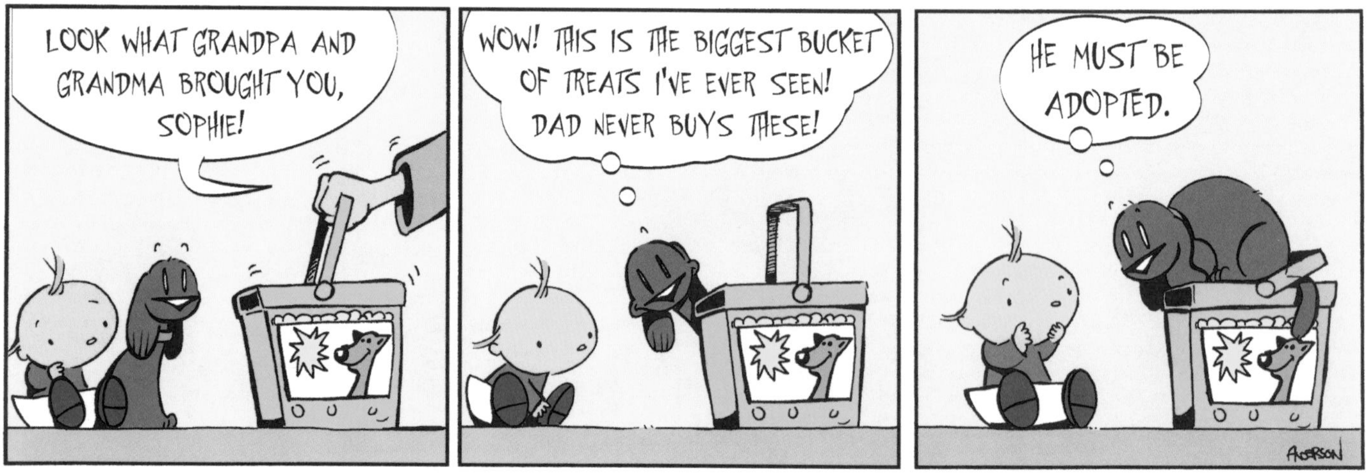
LOOK WHAT GRANDPA AND GRANDMA BROUGHT YOU, SOPHIE!
WOW! THIS IS THE BIGGEST BUCKET OF TREATS I'VE EVER SEEN! DAD NEVER BUYS THESE!
HE MUST BE ADOPTED.
ANDERSON

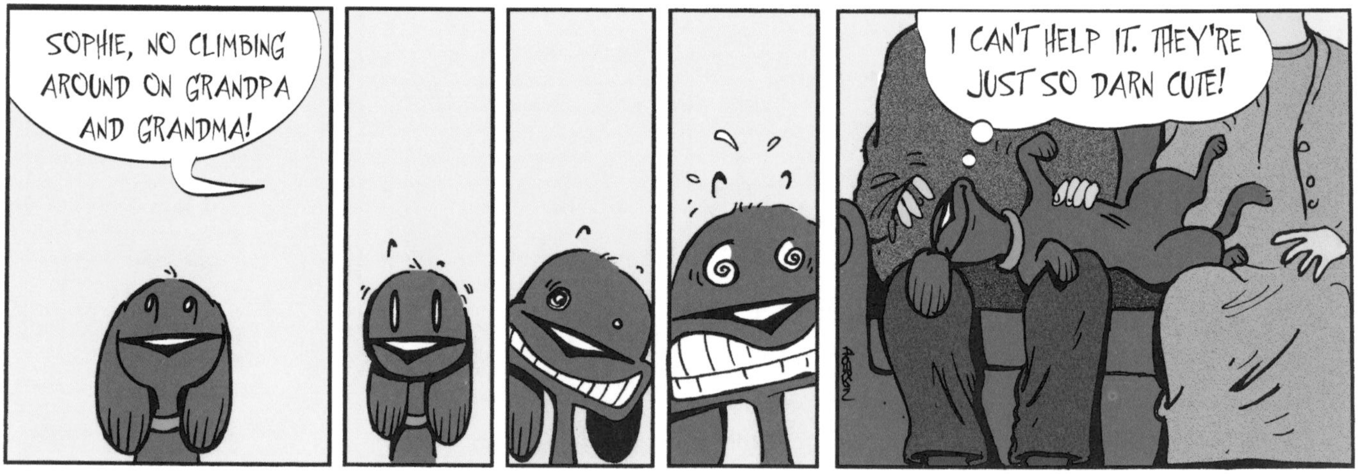
SOPHIE, NO CLIMBING AROUND ON GRANDPA AND GRANDMA!
I CAN'T HELP IT. THEY'RE JUST SO DARN CUTE!

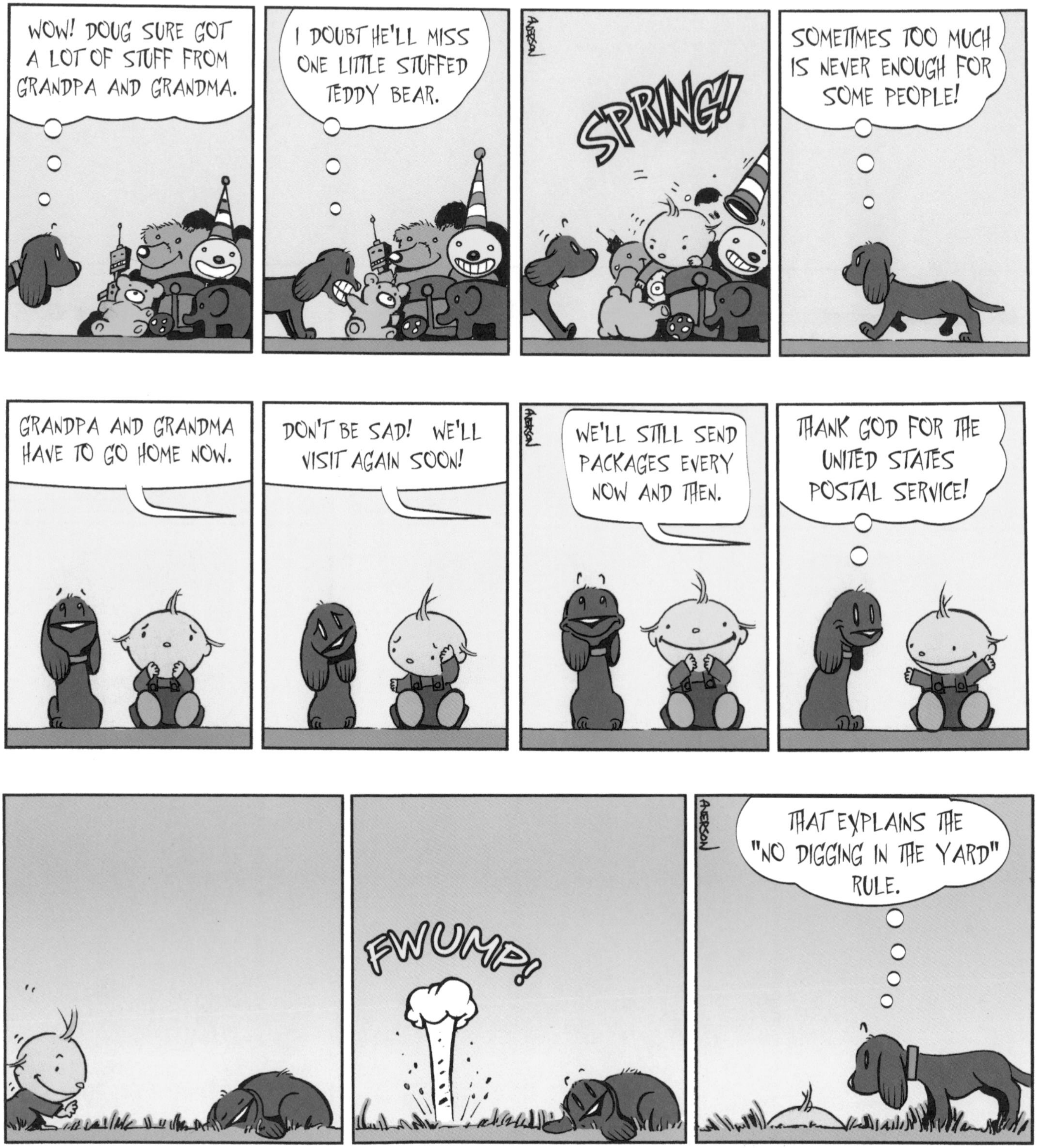
WOW! DOUG SURE GOT A LOT OF STUFF FROM GRANDPA AND GRANDMA.
I DOUBT HE'LL MISS ONE LITTLE STUFFED TEDDY BEAR.
ANDERSON
SPRING!
SOMETIMES TOO MUCH IS NEVER ENOUGH FOR SOME PEOPLE!
GRANDPA AND GRANDMA HAVE TO GO HOME NOW.
DON'T BE SAD! WE'LL VISIT AGAIN SOON!
ANDERSON
WE'LL STILL SEND PACKAGES EVERY NOW AND THEN.
THANK GOD FOR THE UNITED STATES POSTAL SERVICE!
FWUMP!
ANDERSON
THAT EXPLAINS THE "NO DIGGING IN THE YARD" RULE.

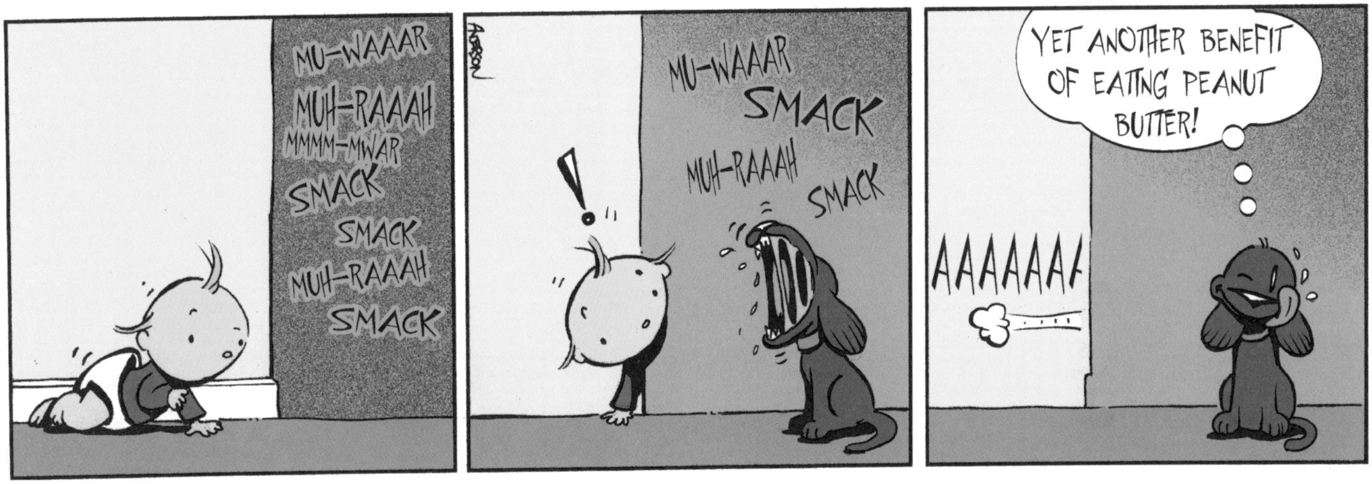
MU-WAAAR
MUH-RAAAH
MMMM-MWAR
SMACK
SMACK
MUH-RAAAH
SMACK
!
MU-WAAAR
SMACK
MUH-RAAAH
SMACK
AAAAAA!
YET ANOTHER BENEFIT OF EATING PEANUT BUTTER!

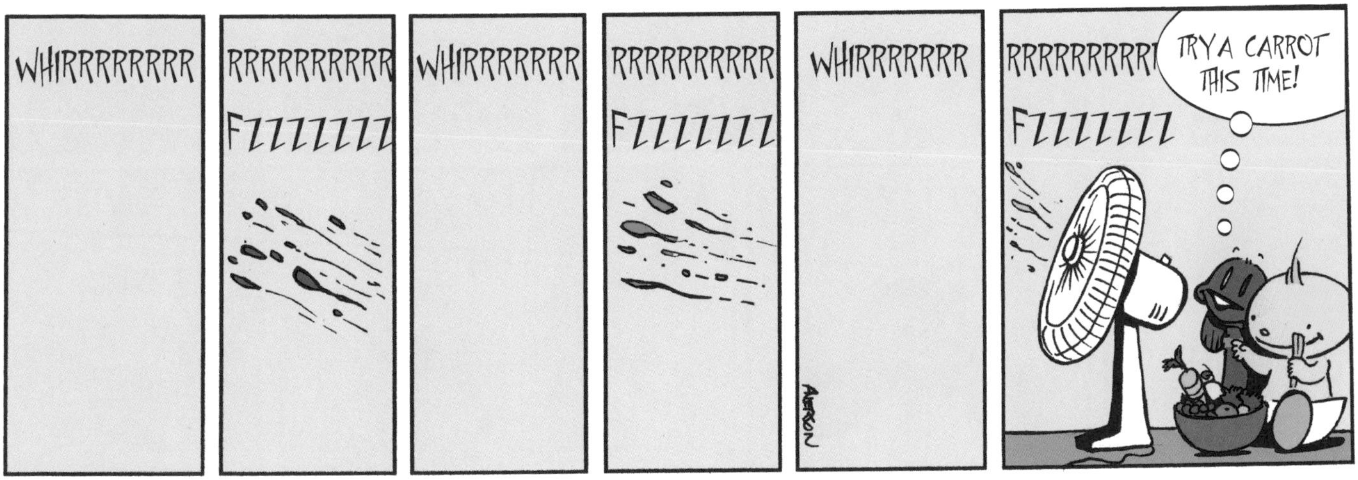
WHIRRRRRRRR
RRRRRRRRRR
FZZZZZZZ
WHIRRRRRRR
RRRRRRRRRR
FZZZZZZZ
WHIRRRRRRR
RRRRRRRRRR
FZZZZZZZ
TRY A CARROT THIS TIME!

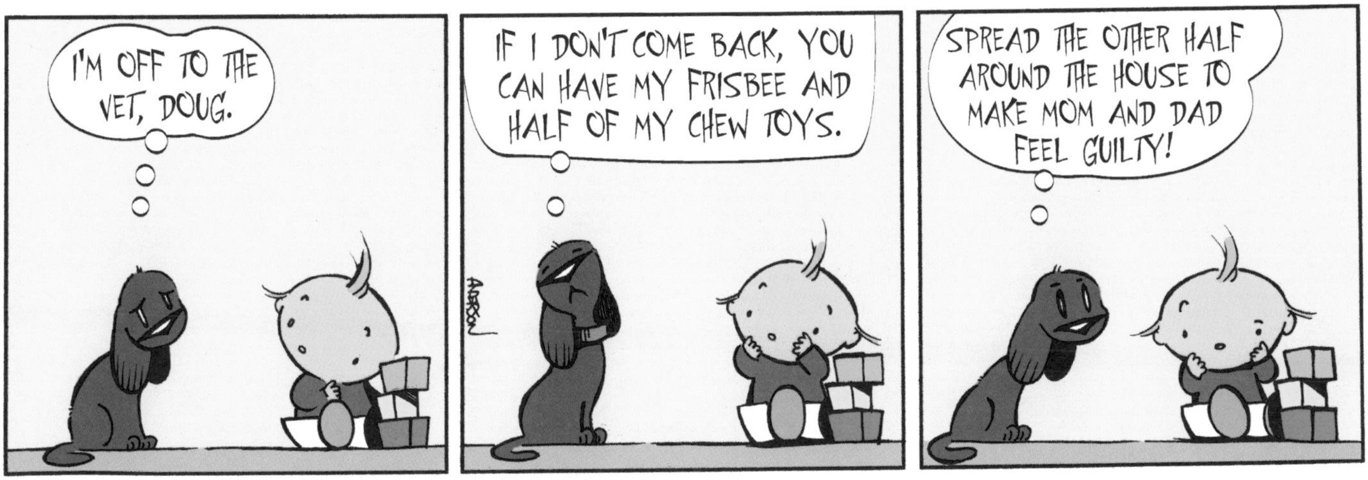
I'M OFF TO THE VET, DOUG.
IF I DON'T COME BACK, YOU CAN HAVE MY FRISBEE AND HALF OF MY CHEW TOYS.
SPREAD THE OTHER HALF AROUND THE HOUSE TO MAKE MOM AND DAD FEEL GUILTY!

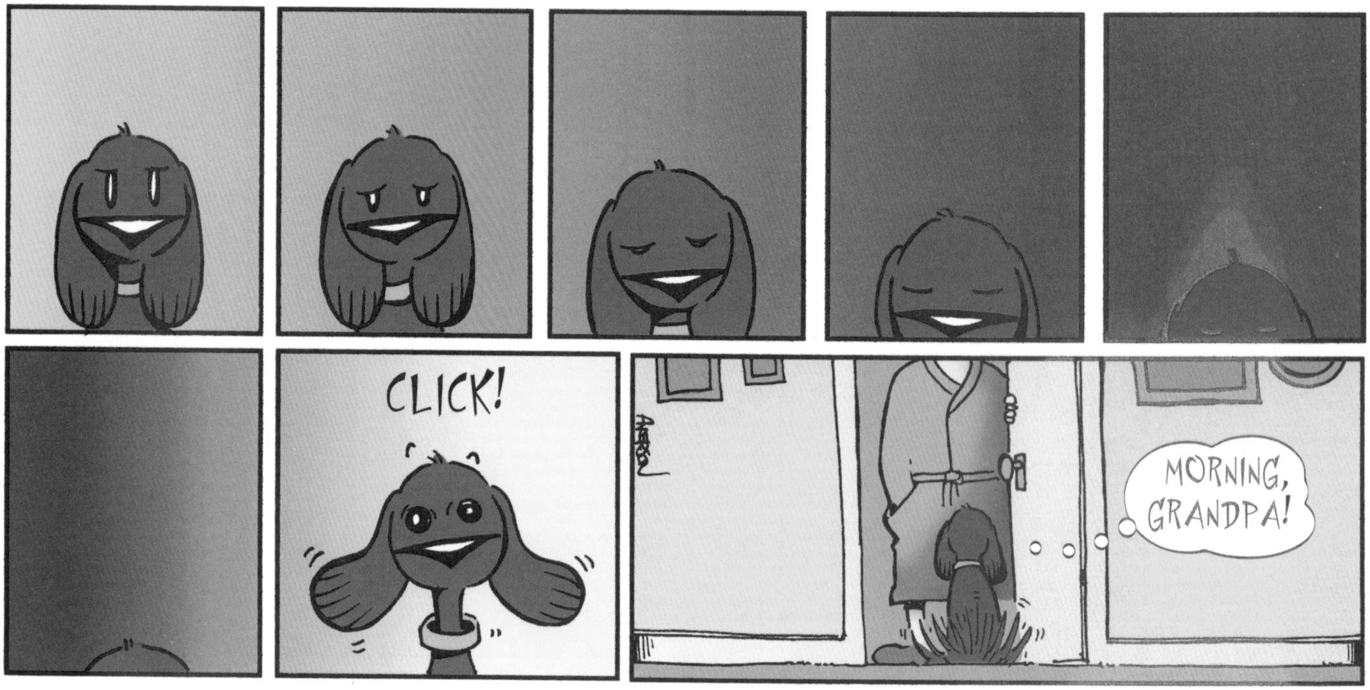
CLICK!
MORNING, GRANDPA!

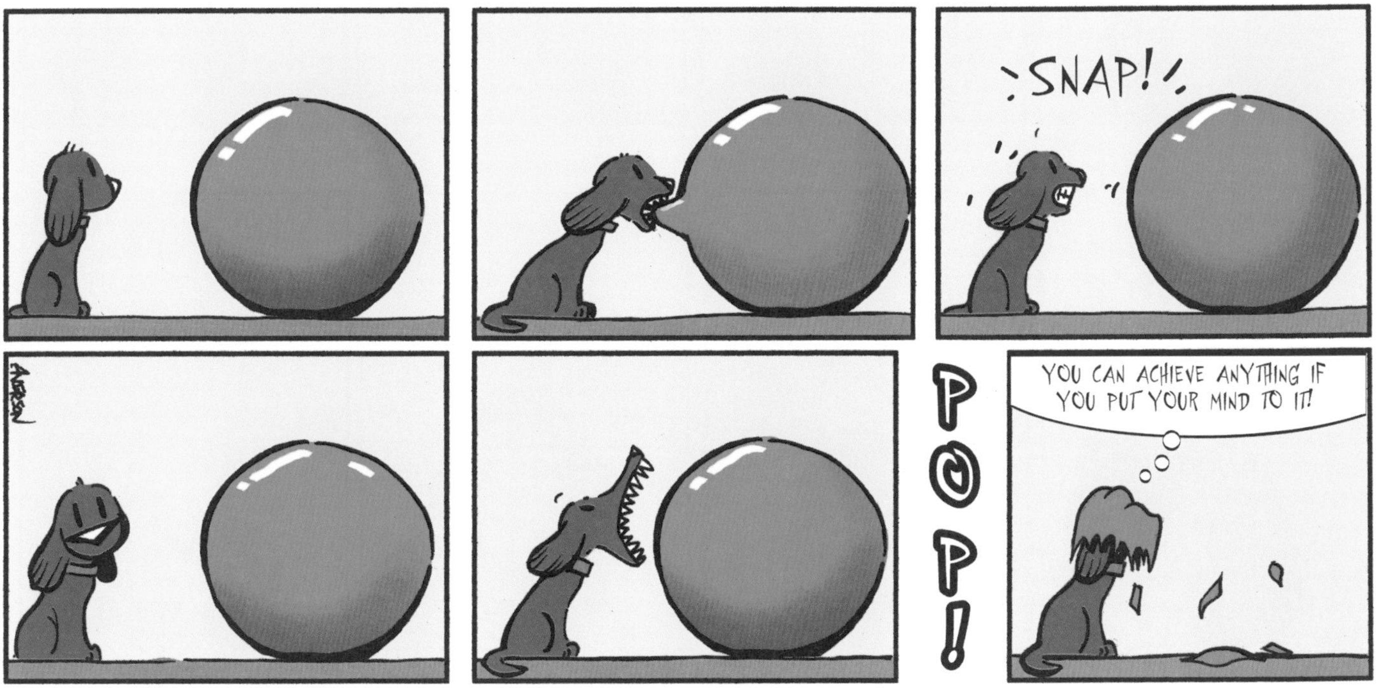
SNAP!
ANDERSON
POP!
YOU CAN ACHIEVE ANYTHING IF YOU PUT YOUR MIND TO IT!

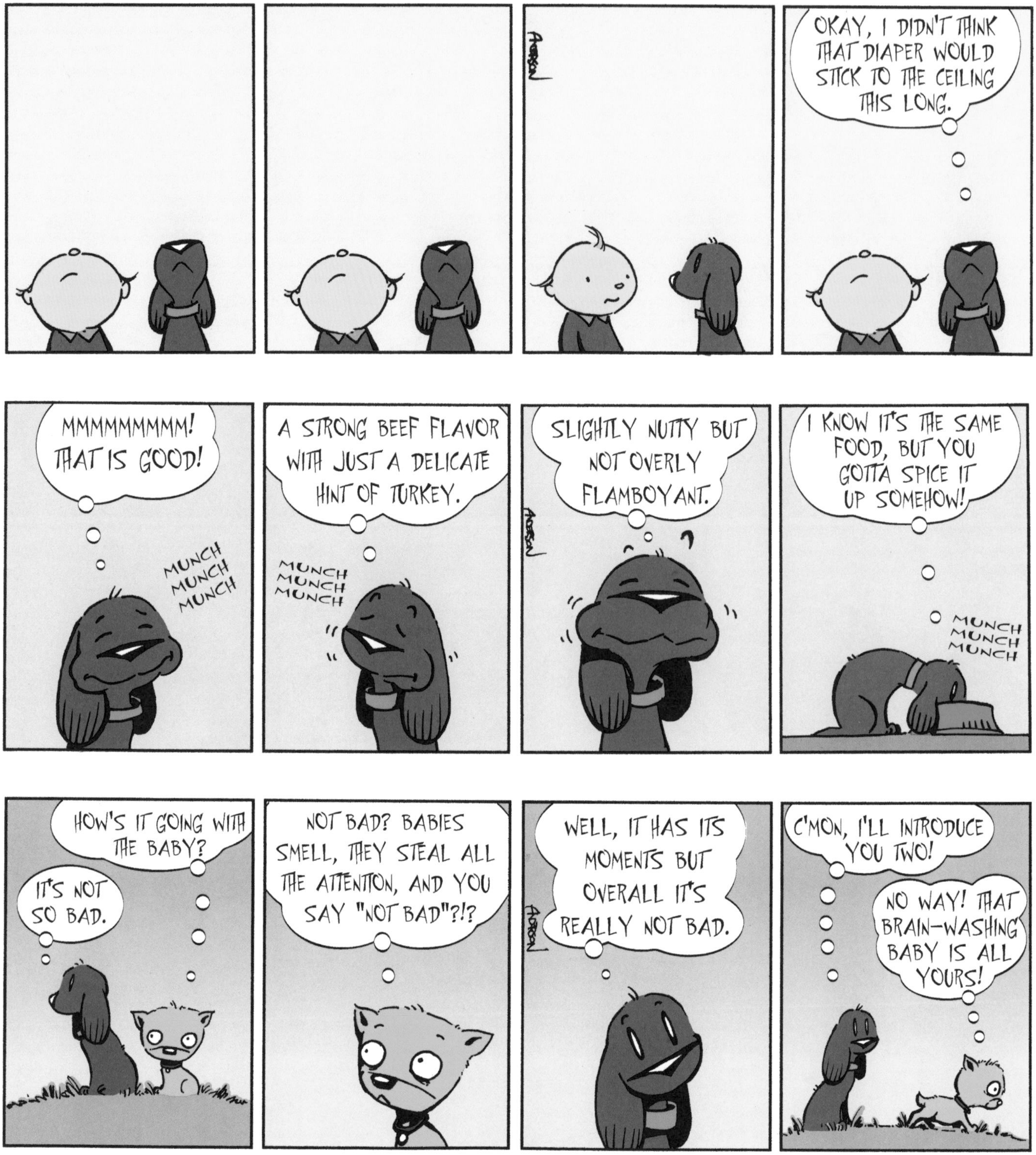
OKAY, I DIDN'T THINK THAT DIAPER WOULD STICK TO THE CEILING THIS LONG.
MMMMMMMMM! THAT IS GOOD!
MUNCH MUNCH MUNCH
A STRONG BEEF FLAVOR WITH JUST A DELICATE HINT OF TURKEY.
MUNCH MUNCH MUNCH
SLIGHTLY NUTTY BUT NOT OVERLY FLAMBOYANT.
I KNOW IT'S THE SAME FOOD, BUT YOU GOTTA SPICE IT UP SOMEHOW!
MUNCH MUNCH MUNCH
HOW'S IT GOING WITH THE BABY?
IT'S NOT SO BAD.
NOT BAD? BABIES SMELL, THEY STEAL ALL THE ATTENTION, AND YOU SAY "NOT BAD"?!?
WELL, IT HAS ITS MOMENTS BUT OVERALL IT'S REALLY NOT BAD.
C'MON, I'LL INTRODUCE YOU TWO!
NO WAY! THAT BRAIN-WASHING BABY IS ALL YOURS!

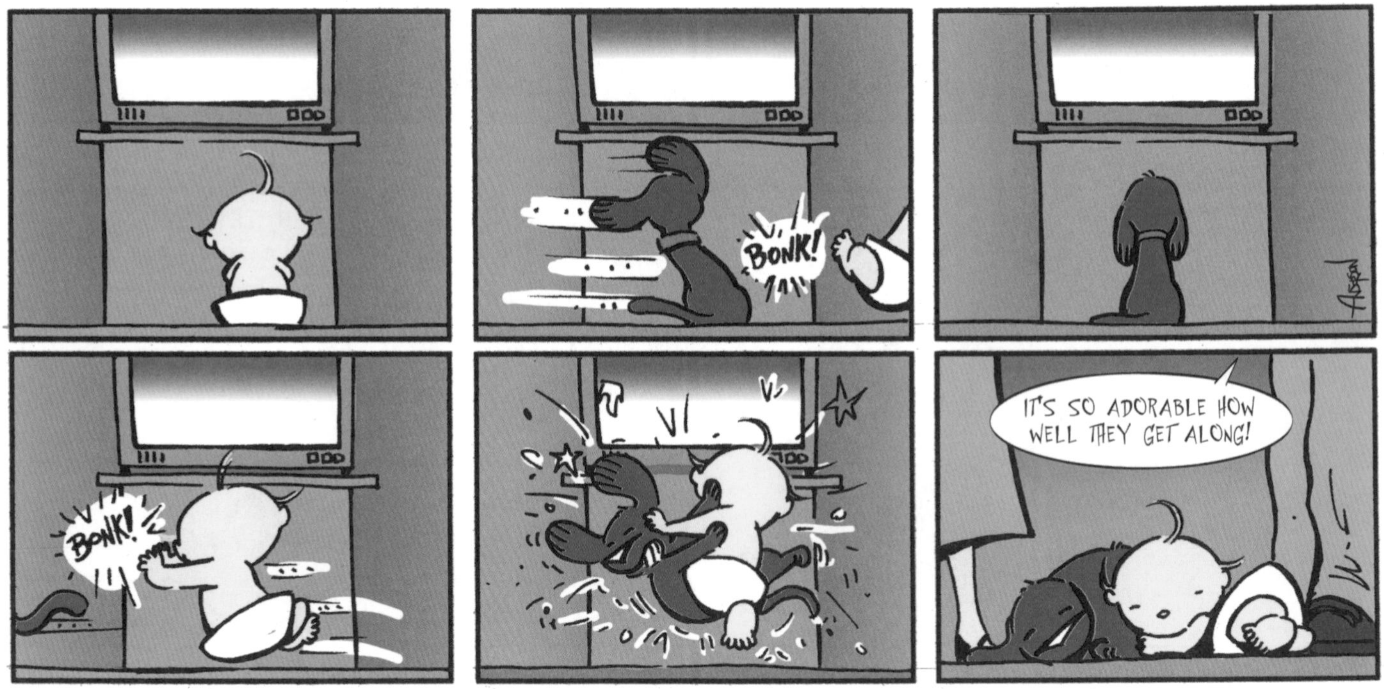
BONK!
BONK!
IT'S SO ADORABLE HOW WELL THEY GET ALONG!

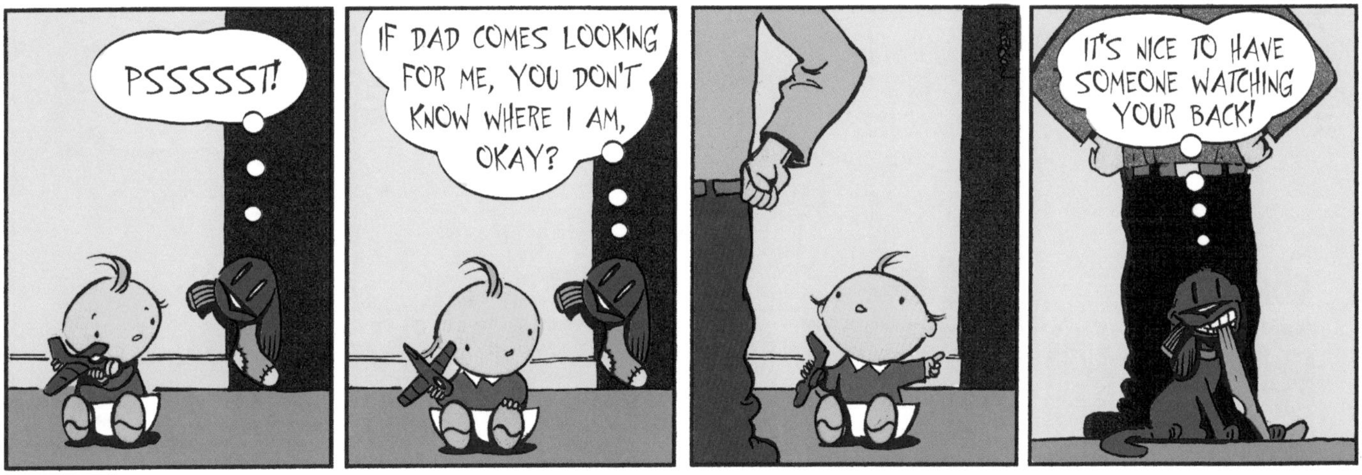
PSSSSST!
IF DAD COMES LOOKING FOR ME, YOU DON'T KNOW WHERE I AM, OKAY?
IT'S NICE TO HAVE SOMEONE WATCHING YOUR BACK!

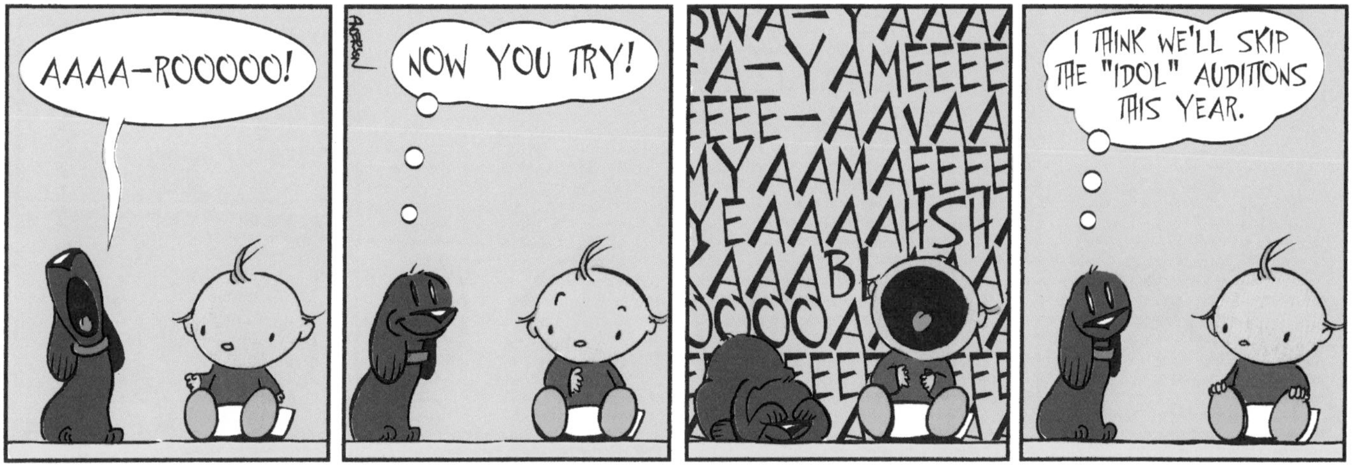
AAAA-ROOOOO!
NOW YOU TRY!
I THINK WE'LL SKIP THE "IDOL" AUDITIONS THIS YEAR.

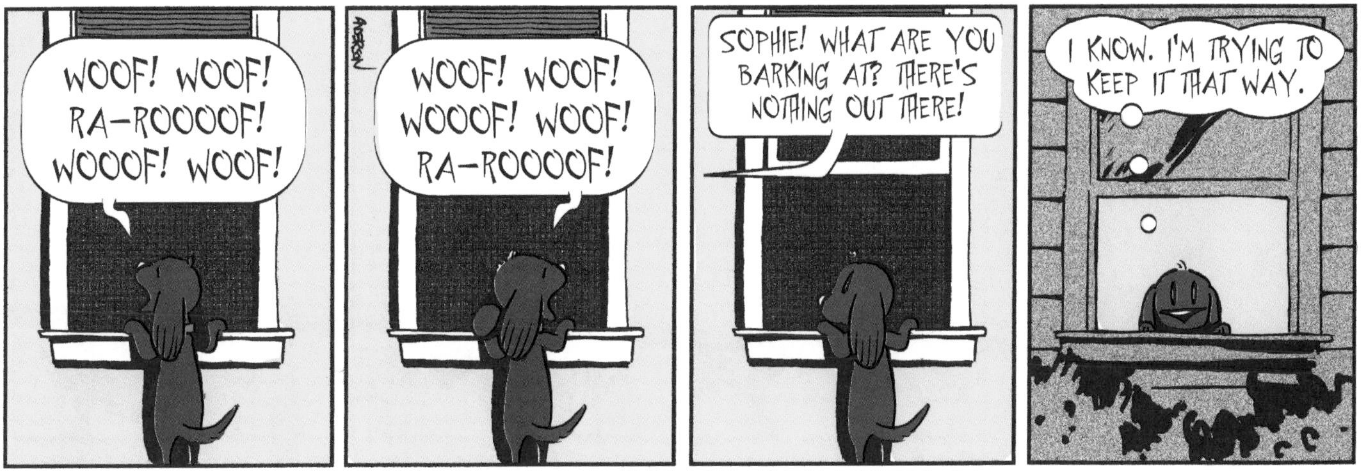
WOOF! WOOF! RA-ROOOOF! WOOOF! WOOF!
WOOF! WOOF! WOOOF! WOOF! RA-ROOOOF!
SOPHIE! WHAT ARE YOU BARKING AT? THERE'S NOTHING OUT THERE!
I KNOW. I'M TRYING TO KEEP IT THAT WAY.

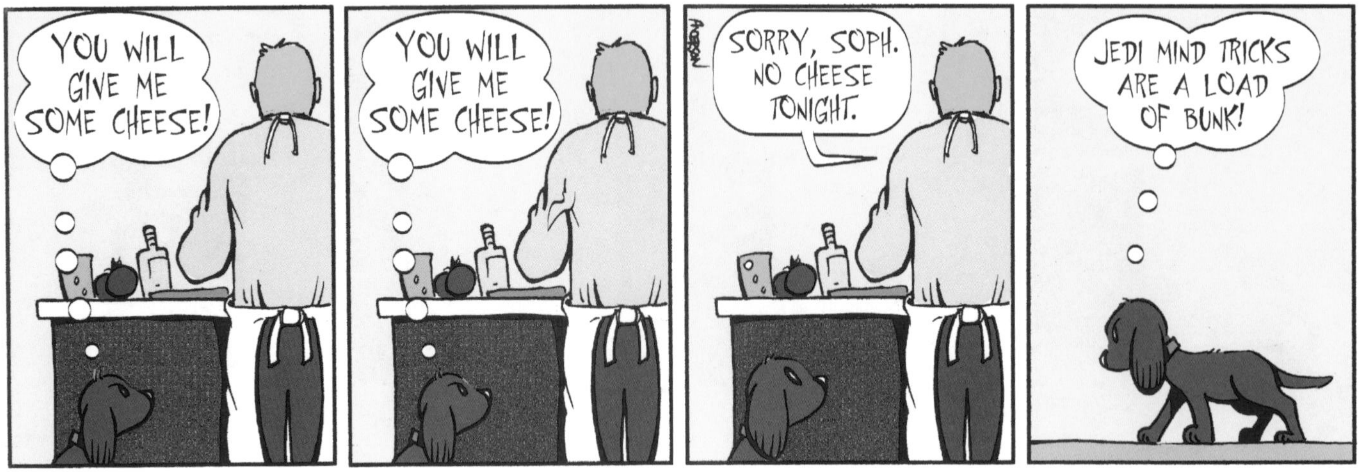
YOU WILL GIVE ME SOME CHEESE!
YOU WILL GIVE ME SOME CHEESE!
SORRY, SOPH. NO CHEESE TONIGHT.
JEDI MIND TRICKS ARE A LOAD OF BUNK!

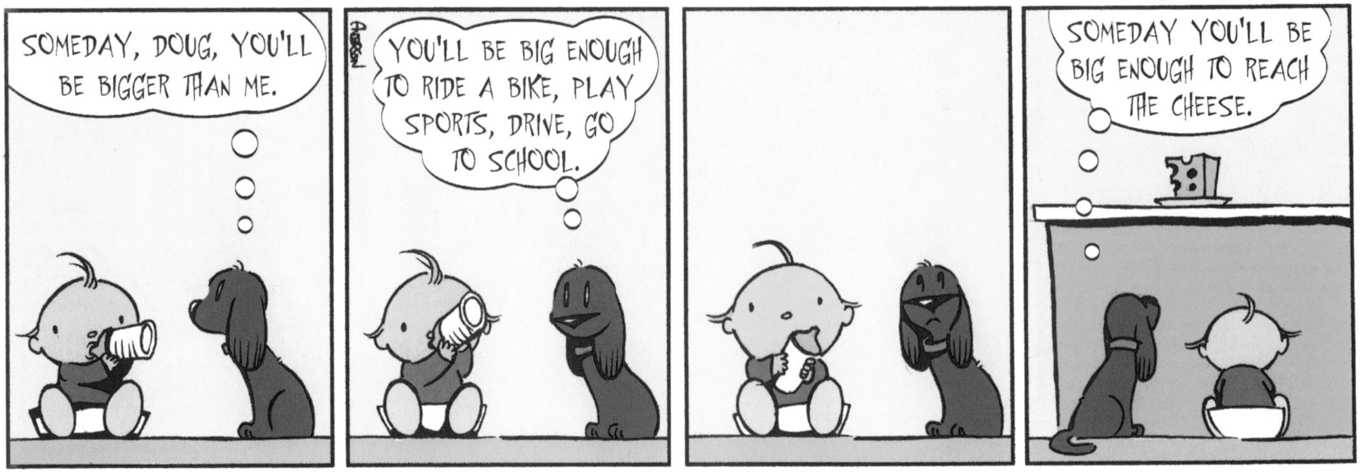
SOMEDAY, DOUG, YOU'LL BE BIGGER THAN ME.
YOU'LL BE BIG ENOUGH TO RIDE A BIKE, PLAY SPORTS, DRIVE, GO TO SCHOOL.
SOMEDAY YOU'LL BE BIG ENOUGH TO REACH THE CHEESE.

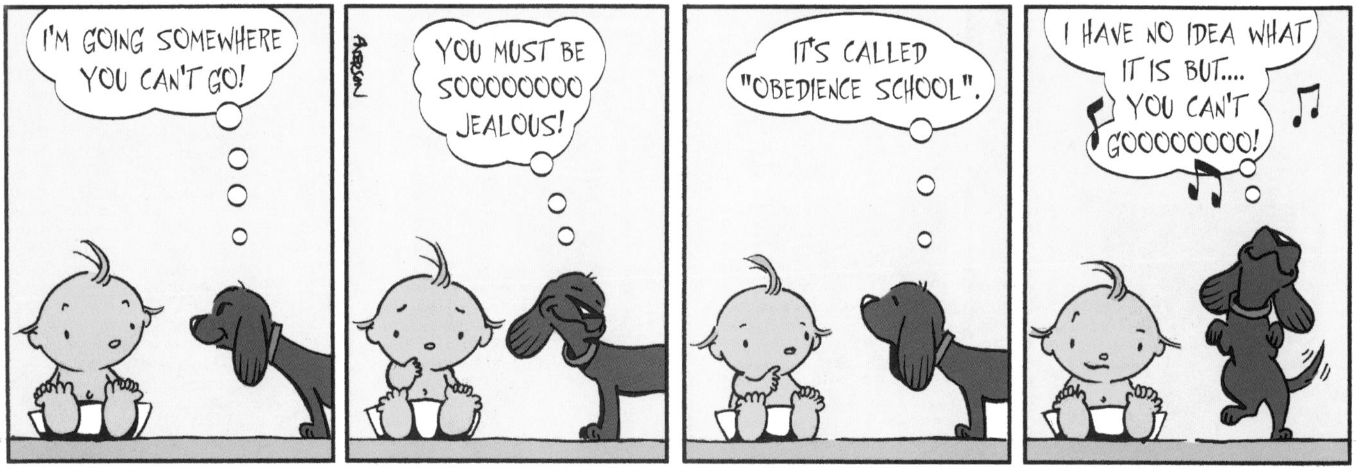
I'M GOING SOMEWHERE YOU CAN'T GO!
YOU MUST BE SOOOOOOOOO JEALOUS!
IT'S CALLED "OBEDIENCE SCHOOL".
I HAVE NO IDEA WHAT IT IS BUT.... YOU CAN'T GOOOOOOOO!

WELCOME TO OBEDIENCE 101.

FIRST WE'LL WORK ON OUR "STAY" COMMANDS.

THEN WE WILL MOVE ON TO OUR "SITS" AND "DOWNS".

ME AND THE BOXER ARE GOING TO MAKE A BREAK FOR IT. YOU WITH US?

DOG DAY TRAINING

JACQUES, COME!

MAYBE YOU SHOULD LISTEN TO YOUR MOM.

NO!

NOTHING CAN BREAK MY WILL! NOT HER, NOT ANYTHING!

I HAVE A TREAT FOR YOU!

HIS FORTITUDE IS BREATHTAKING!

ZIP!

DOG DAY TRAINING

SOPHIE, STAY!

DOG DAY TRAINING

STAAAAAAY! GOOD GIRL!

DOG DA TRAINI

OKAY, SOPHIE, COME!

SOPHIE, COME! C'MON!

DOG DAY TRAINING

Z

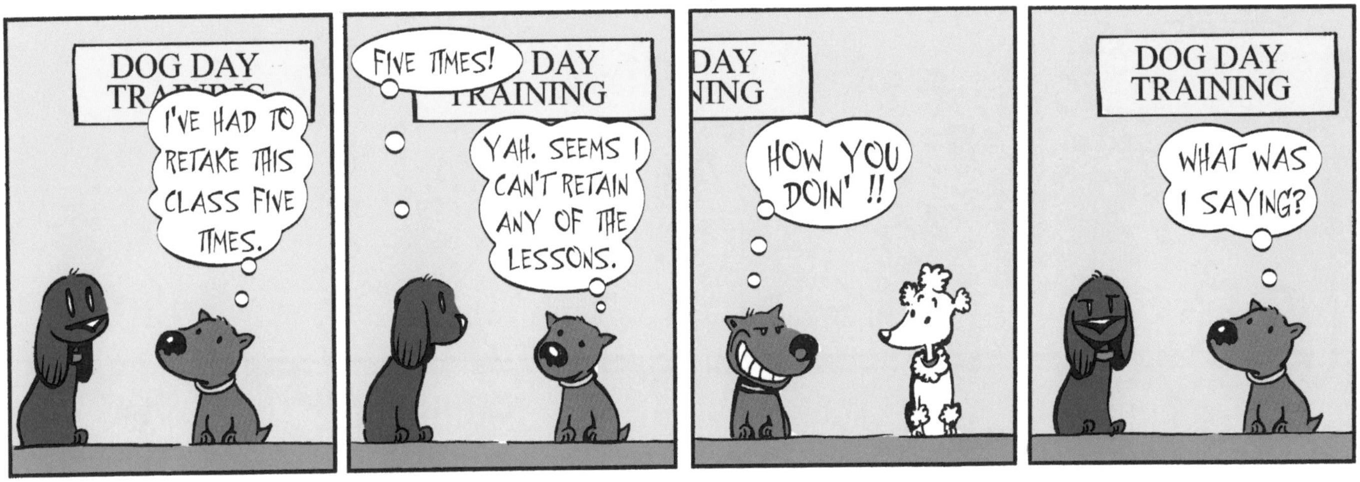
DOG DAY TRAINING
I'VE HAD TO RETAKE THIS CLASS FIVE TIMES.
FIVE TIMES!
YAH. SEEMS I CAN'T RETAIN ANY OF THE LESSONS.
HOW YOU DOIN' !!
DOG DAY TRAINING
WHAT WAS I SAYING?

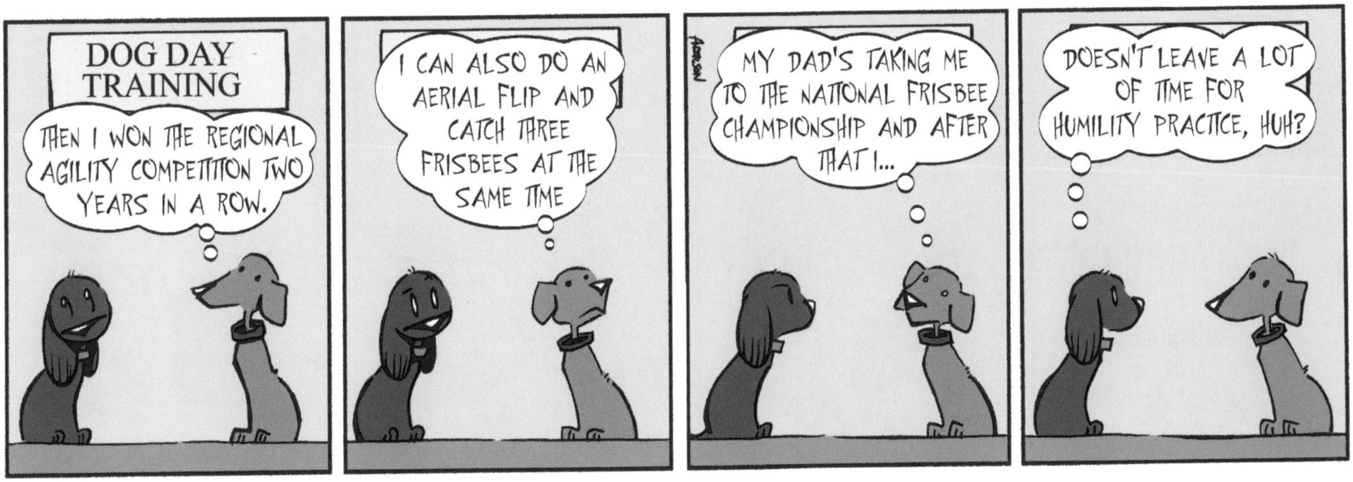
DOG DAY TRAINING
THEN I WON THE REGIONAL AGILITY COMPETITION TWO YEARS IN A ROW.
I CAN ALSO DO AN AERIAL FLIP AND CATCH THREE FRISBEES AT THE SAME TIME
MY DAD'S TAKING ME TO THE NATIONAL FRISBEE CHAMPIONSHIP AND AFTER THAT I...
DOESN'T LEAVE A LOT OF TIME FOR HUMILITY PRACTICE, HUH?

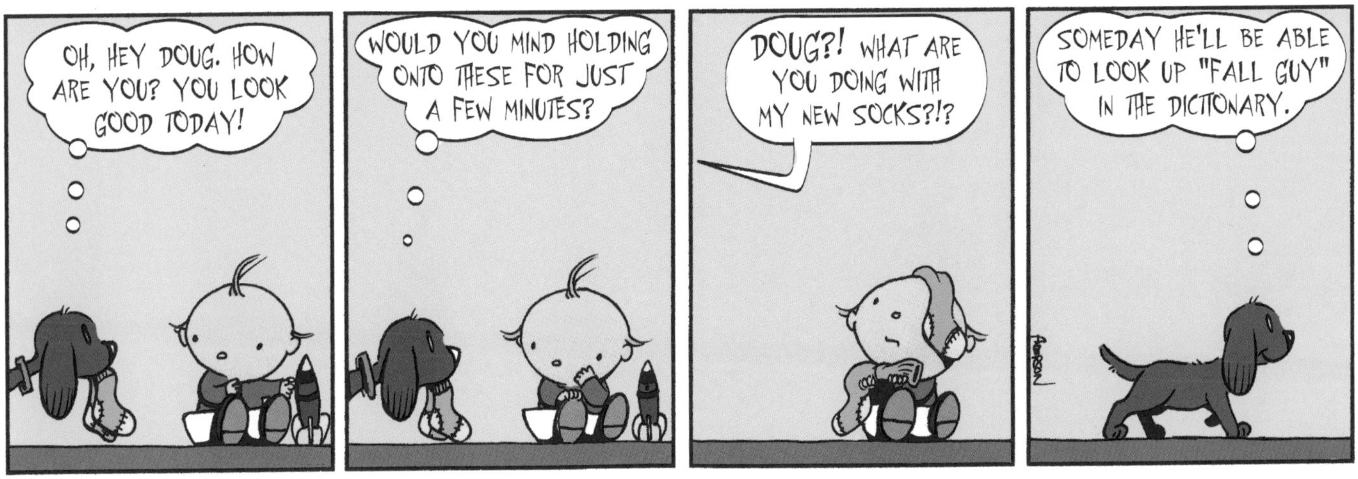
OH, HEY DOUG. HOW ARE YOU? YOU LOOK GOOD TODAY!
WOULD YOU MIND HOLDING ONTO THESE FOR JUST A FEW MINUTES?
DOUG?! WHAT ARE YOU DOING WITH MY NEW SOCKS?!?
SOMEDAY HE'LL BE ABLE TO LOOK UP "FALL GUY" IN THE DICTIONARY.

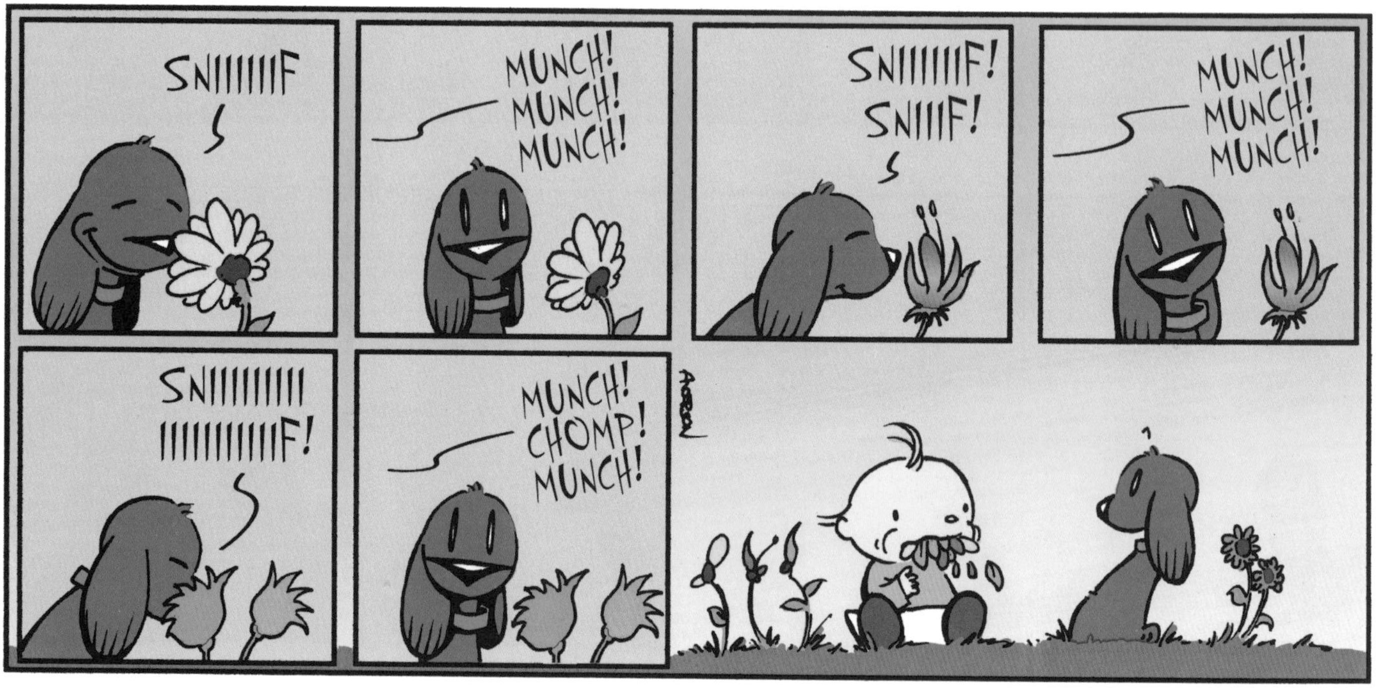
SNIIIIIIF
MUNCH! MUNCH! MUNCH!
SNIIIIIIF! SNIIIF!
MUNCH! MUNCH! MUNCH!
SNIIIIIIIIII IIIIIIIIIIIF!
MUNCH! CHOMP! MUNCH!

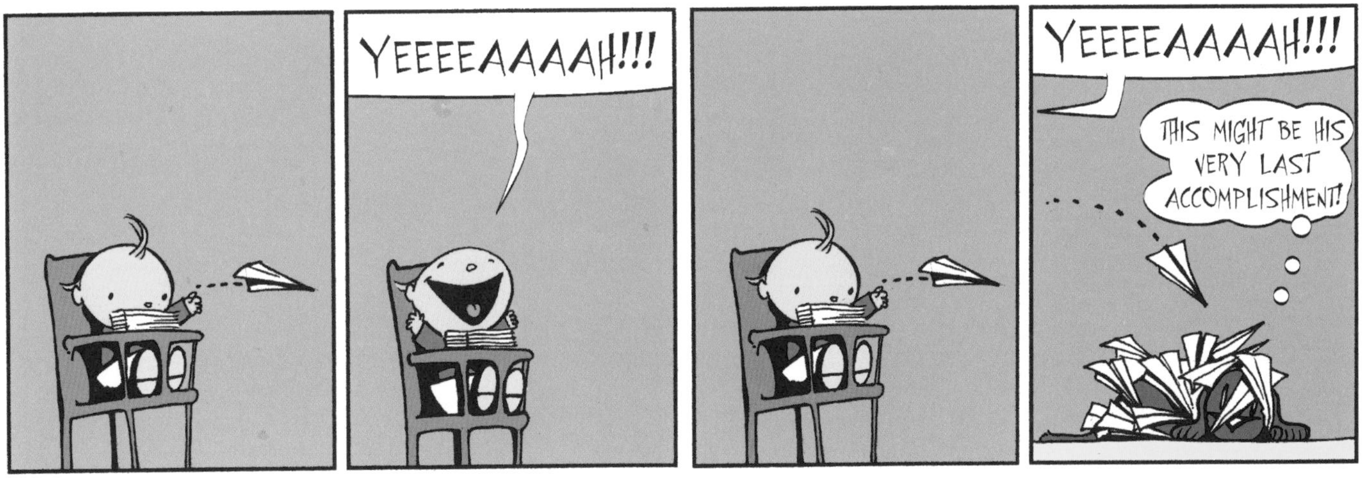
YEEEEAAAAH!!!
YEEEEAAAAH!!!
THIS MIGHT BE HIS VERY LAST ACCOMPLISHMENT!

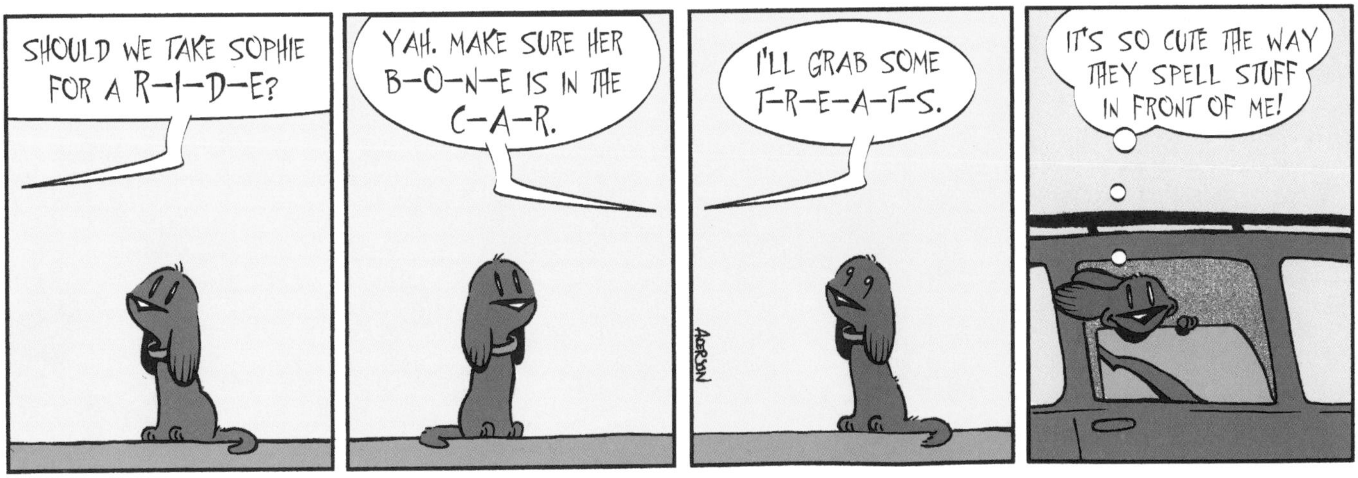
SHOULD WE TAKE SOPHIE FOR A R—I—D—E?
YAH. MAKE SURE HER B—O—N—E IS IN THE C—A—R.
I'LL GRAB SOME T—R—E—A—T—S.
IT'S SO CUTE THE WAY THEY SPELL STUFF IN FRONT OF ME!

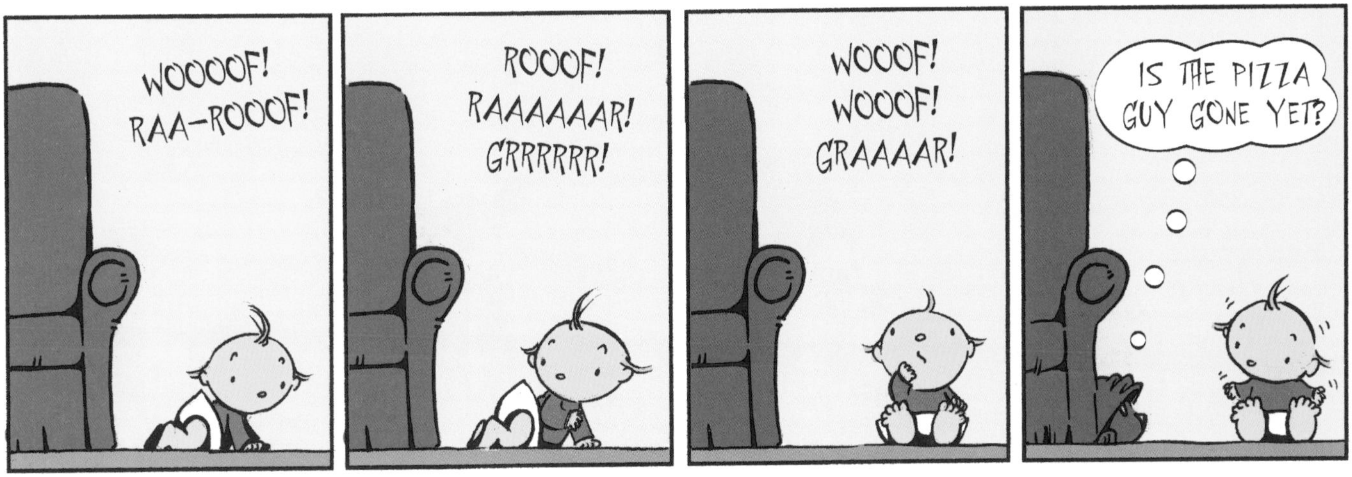
WOOOOF! RAA—ROOOF!
ROOOF! RAAAAAAR! GRRRRRR!
WOOOF! WOOOF! GRAAAAR!
IS THE PIZZA GUY GONE YET?

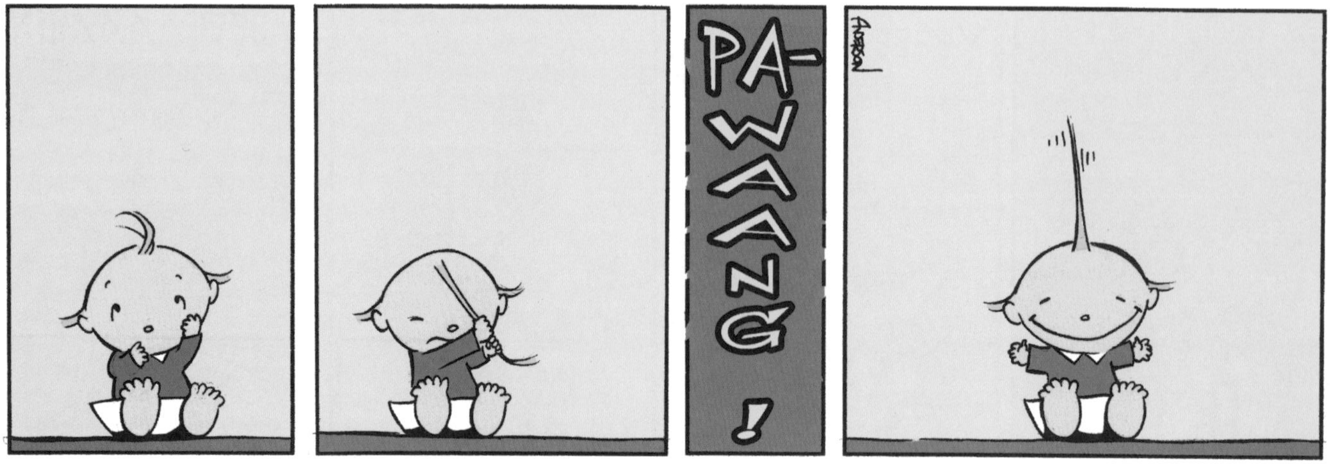
PA-WAAANG!

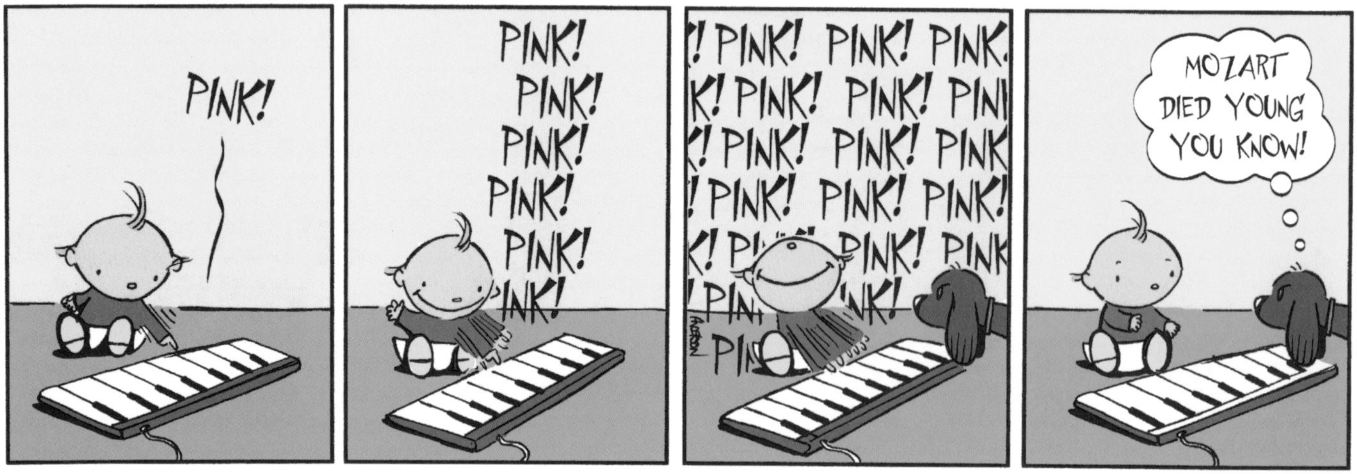
PINK!
PINK! PINK! PINK! PINK! PINK!
PINK! PINK!
PINK! PINK!
PINK! PINK!
PINK! PINK!
MOZART DIED YOUNG YOU KNOW!

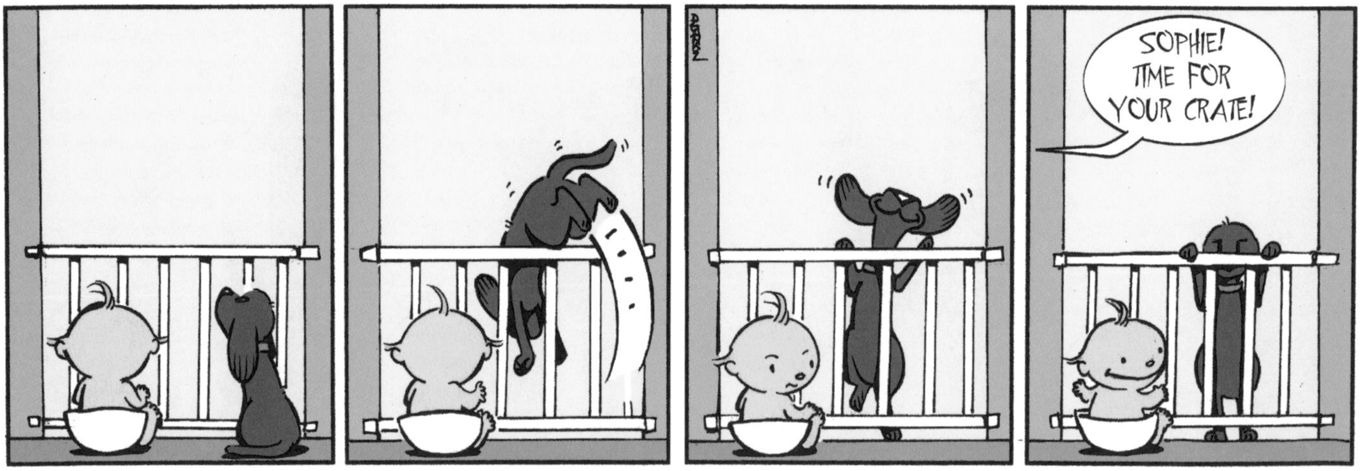
SOPHIE! TIME FOR YOUR CRATE!

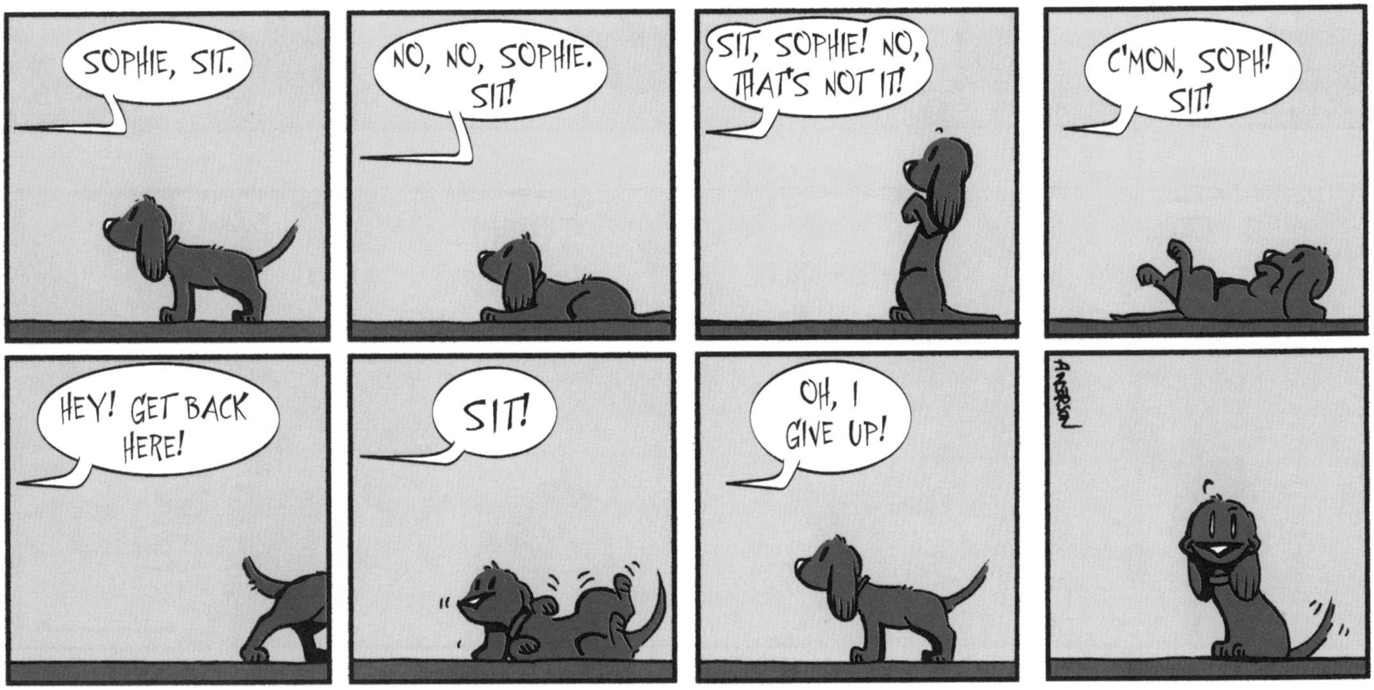
SOPHIE, SIT.
NO, NO, SOPHIE. SIT!
SIT, SOPHIE! NO, THAT'S NOT IT!
C'MON, SOPH! SIT!
HEY! GET BACK HERE!
SIT!
OH, I GIVE UP!
ANDERSON

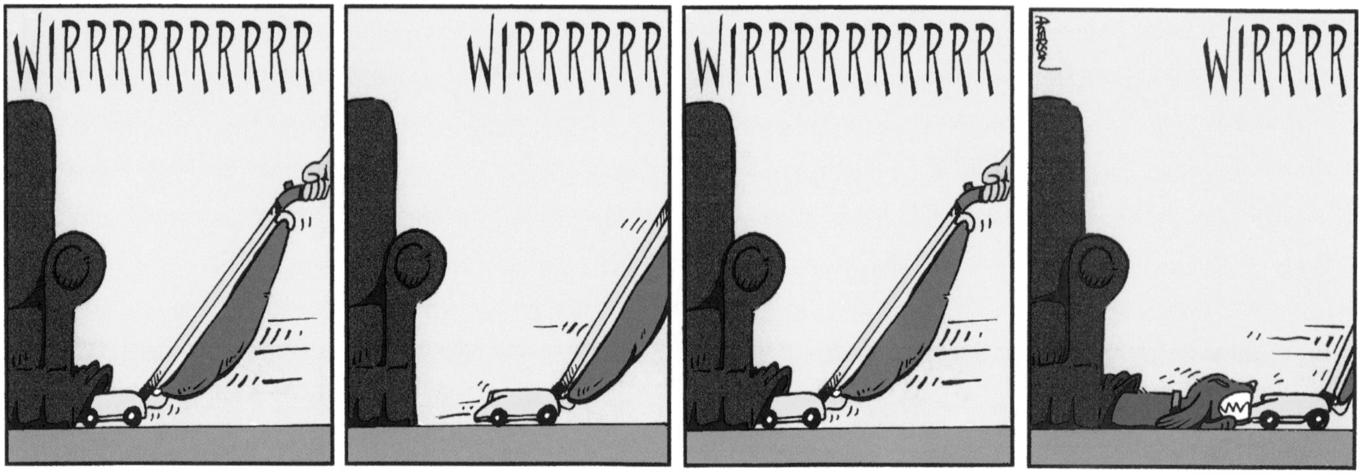
WIRRRRRRRRRR
WIRRRRRR
WIRRRRRRRRRRR
WIRRRR

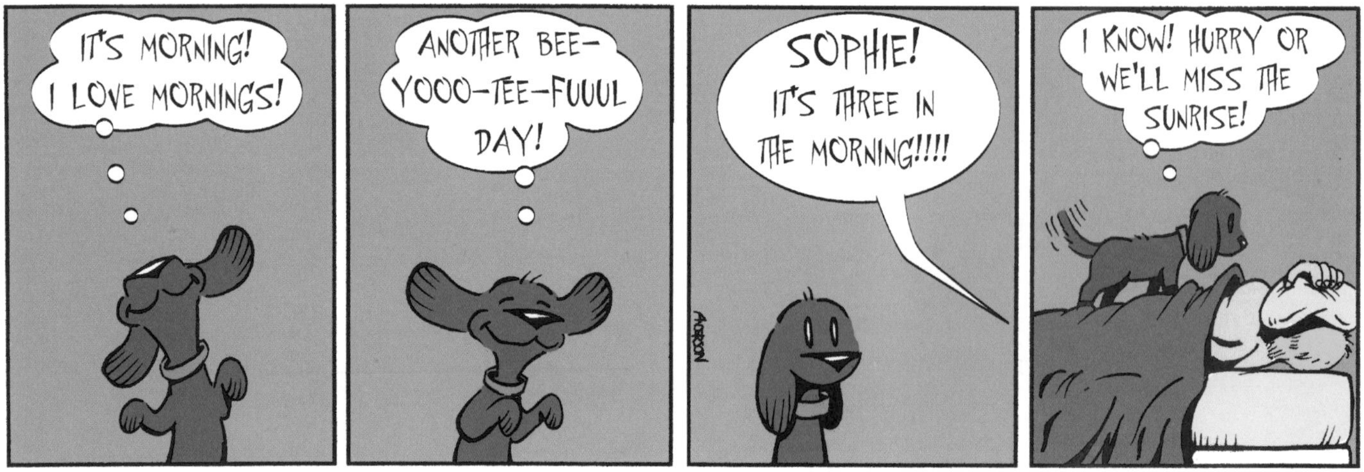
IT'S MORNING! I LOVE MORNINGS!
ANOTHER BEE-YOOO-TEE-FUUUL DAY!
SOPHIE! IT'S THREE IN THE MORNING!!!!
I KNOW! HURRY OR WE'LL MISS THE SUNRISE!

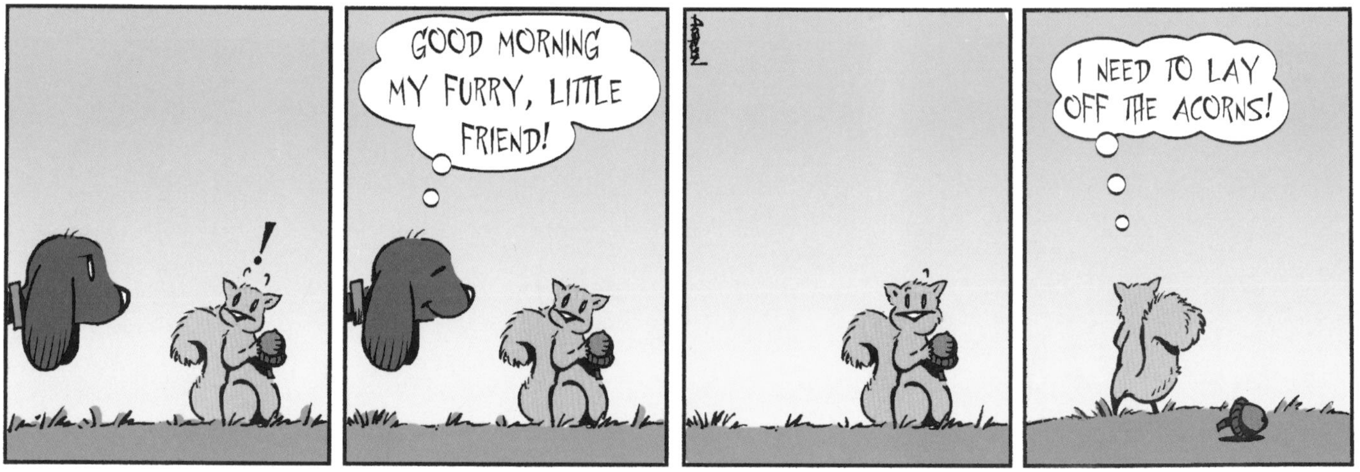
!
GOOD MORNING MY FURRY, LITTLE FRIEND!
I NEED TO LAY OFF THE ACORNS!

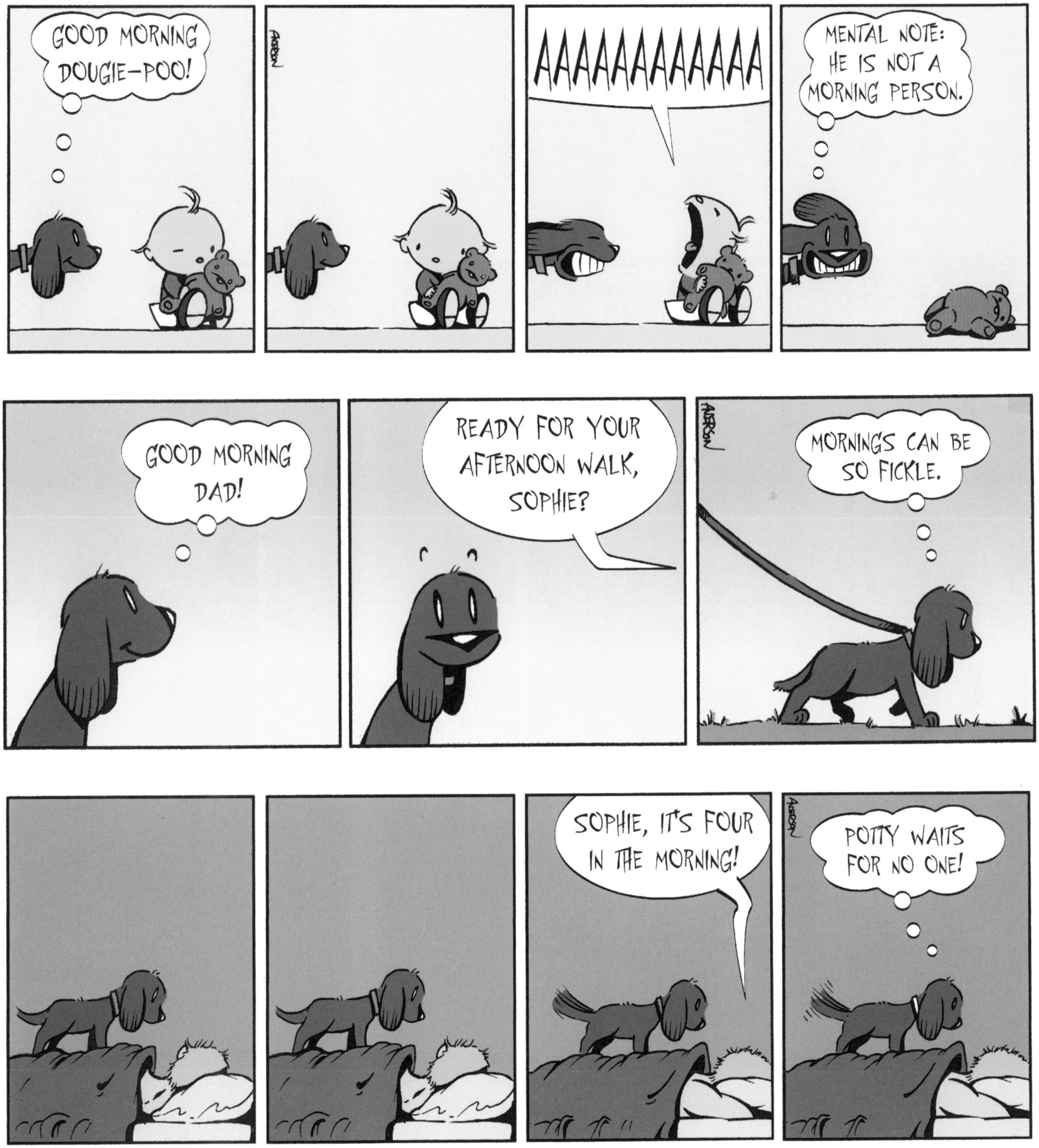
GOOD MORNING DOUGIE-POO!
AAAAAAAAAAAA
MENTAL NOTE: HE IS NOT A MORNING PERSON.
GOOD MORNING DAD!
READY FOR YOUR AFTERNOON WALK, SOPHIE?
MORNINGS CAN BE SO FICKLE.
SOPHIE, IT'S FOUR IN THE MORNING!
POTTY WAITS FOR NO ONE!

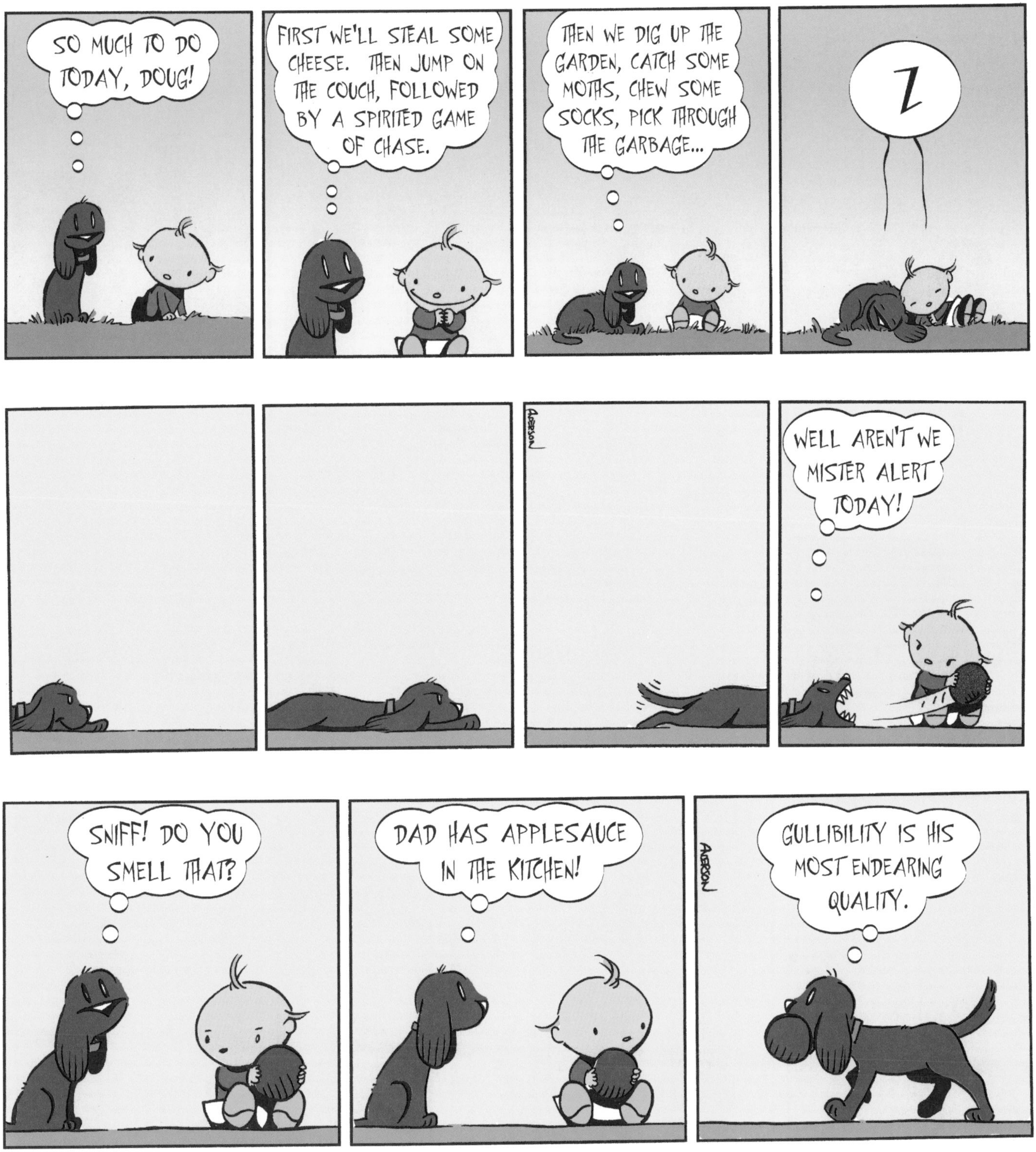
SO MUCH TO DO TODAY, DOUG!
FIRST WE'LL STEAL SOME CHEESE. THEN JUMP ON THE COUCH, FOLLOWED BY A SPIRITED GAME OF CHASE.
THEN WE DIG UP THE GARDEN, CATCH SOME MOTHS, CHEW SOME SOCKS, PICK THROUGH THE GARBAGE...
Z
ANDERSON
WELL AREN'T WE MISTER ALERT TODAY!
SNIFF! DO YOU SMELL THAT?
DAD HAS APPLESAUCE IN THE KITCHEN!
ANDERSON
GULLIBILITY IS HIS MOST ENDEARING QUALITY.

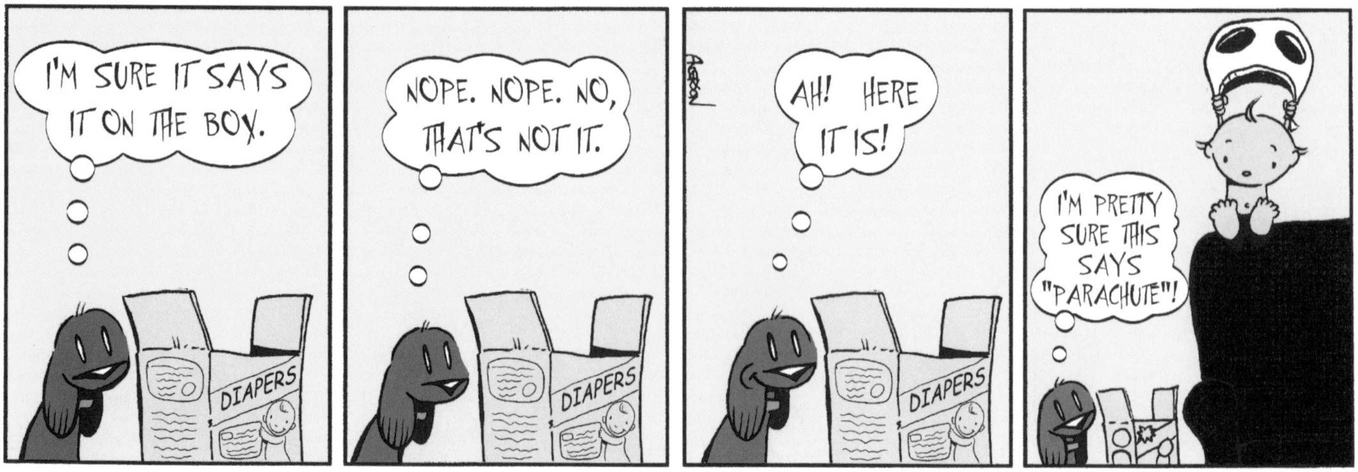
I'M SURE IT SAYS IT ON THE BOX.
NOPE. NOPE. NO, THAT'S NOT IT.
AH! HERE IT IS!
DIAPERS
I'M PRETTY SURE THIS SAYS "PARACHUTE"!

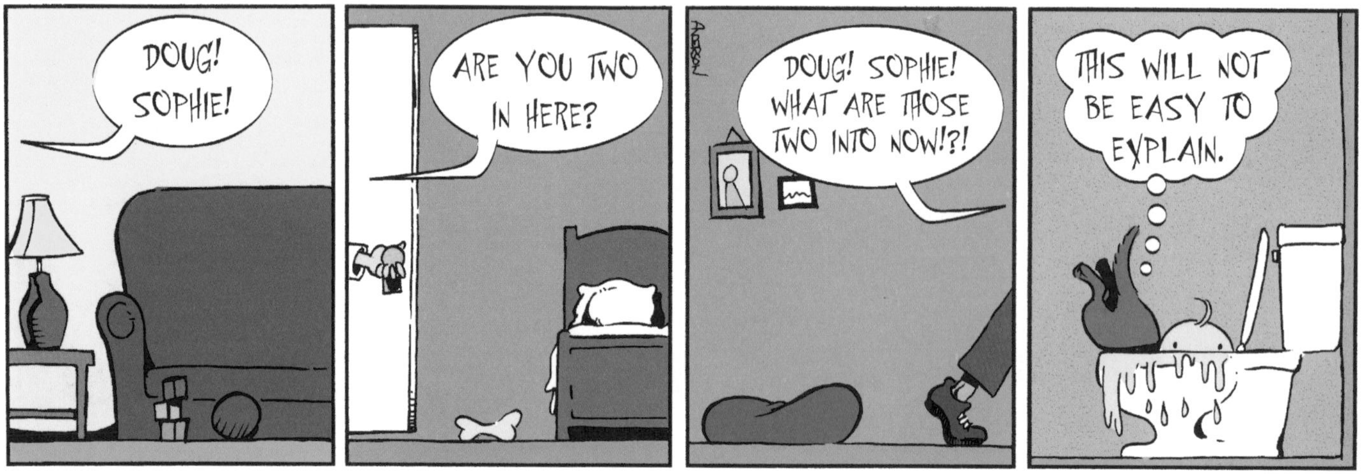
DOUG! SOPHIE!
ARE YOU TWO IN HERE?
DOUG! SOPHIE! WHAT ARE THOSE TWO INTO NOW!?!
THIS WILL NOT BE EASY TO EXPLAIN.

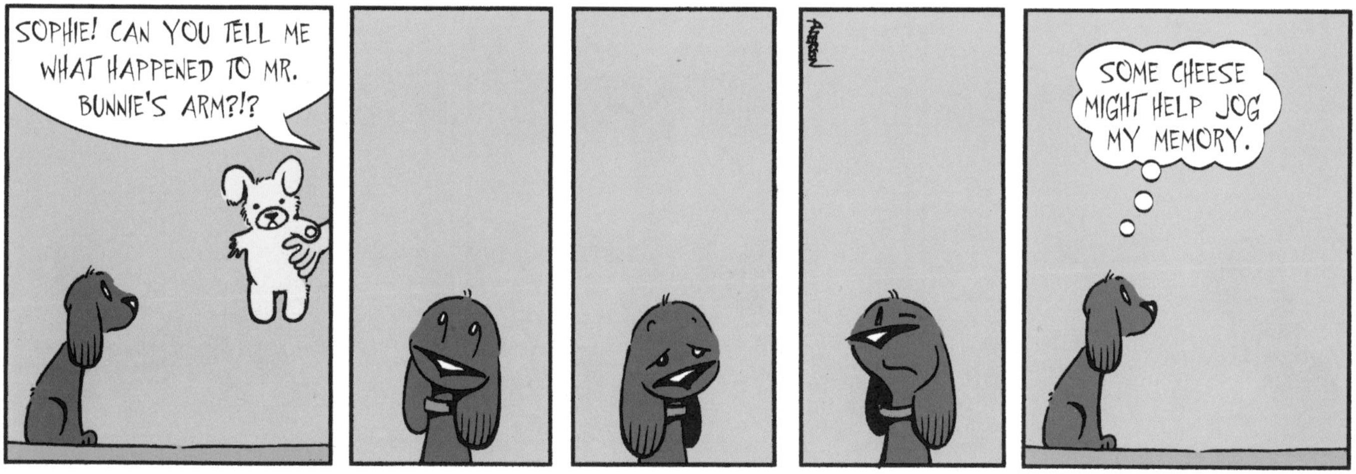
SOPHIE! CAN YOU TELL ME WHAT HAPPENED TO MR. BUNNIE'S ARM?!?
SOME CHEESE MIGHT HELP JOG MY MEMORY.

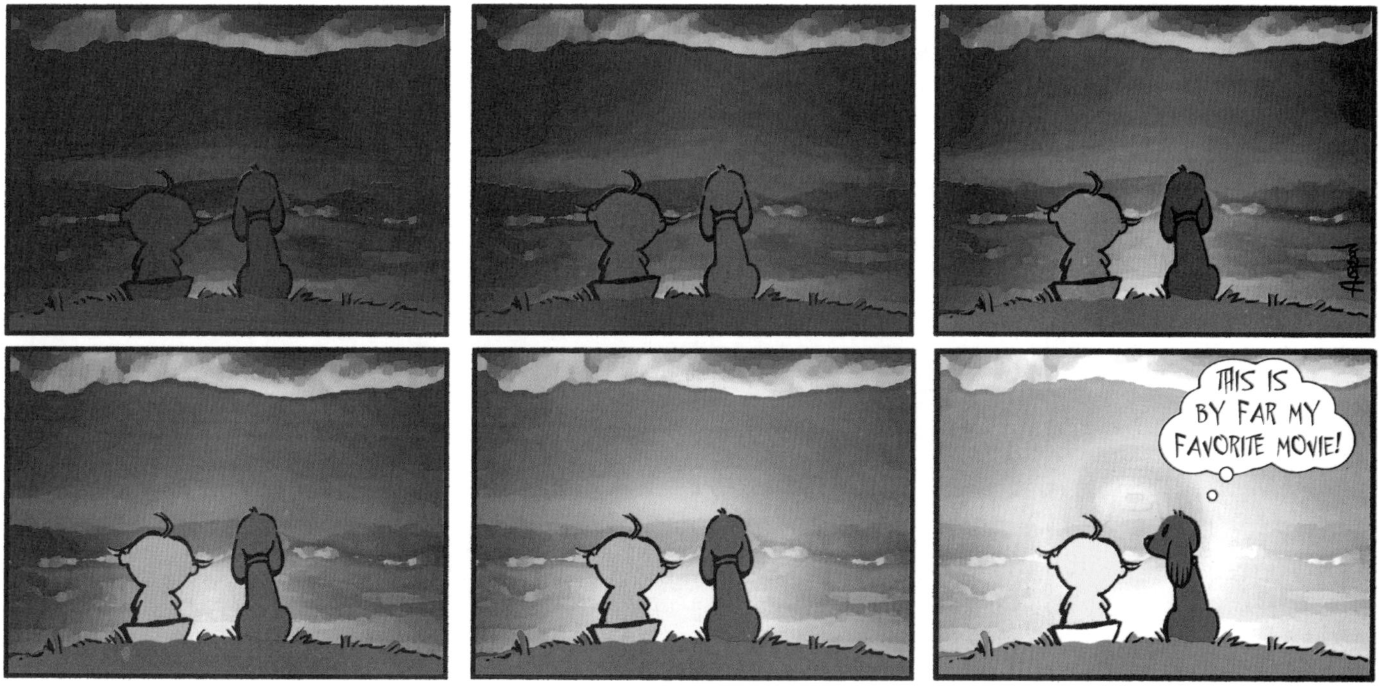
THIS IS BY FAR MY FAVORITE MOVIE!

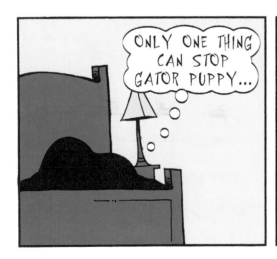

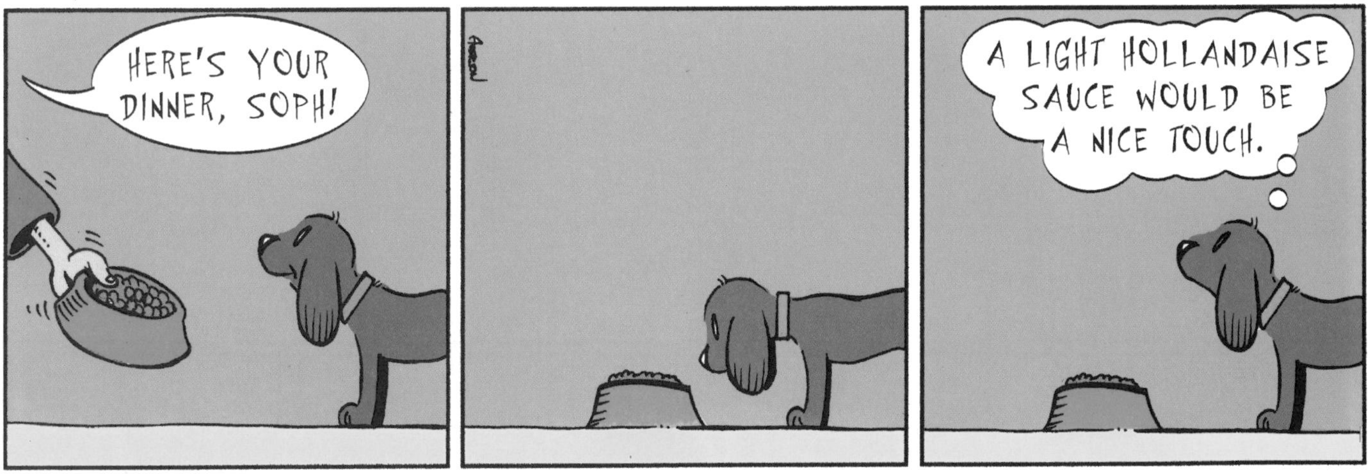
HERE'S YOUR DINNER, SOPH!
A LIGHT HOLLANDAISE SAUCE WOULD BE A NICE TOUCH.

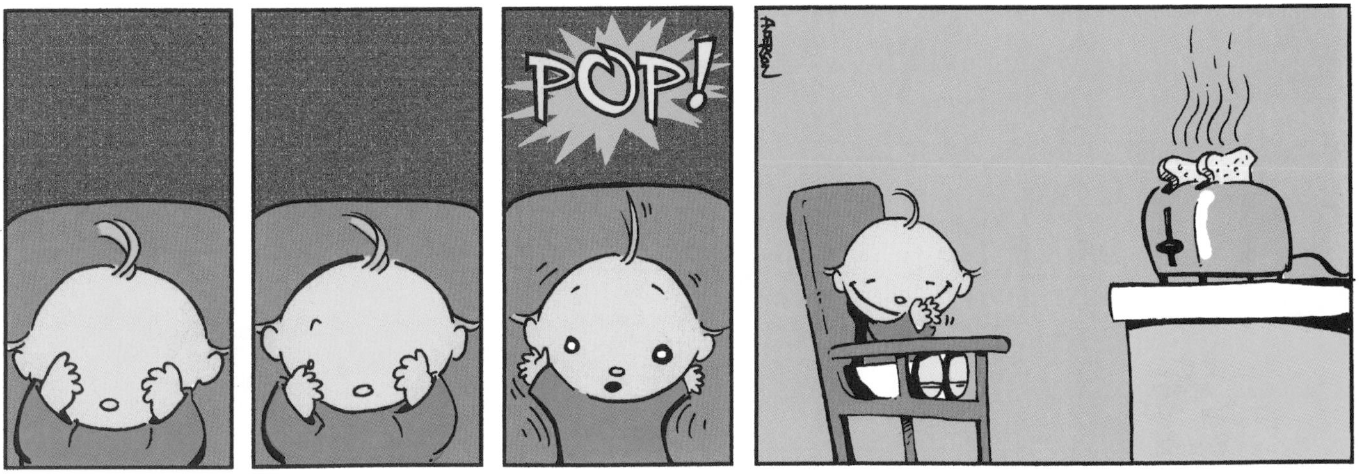
POP!

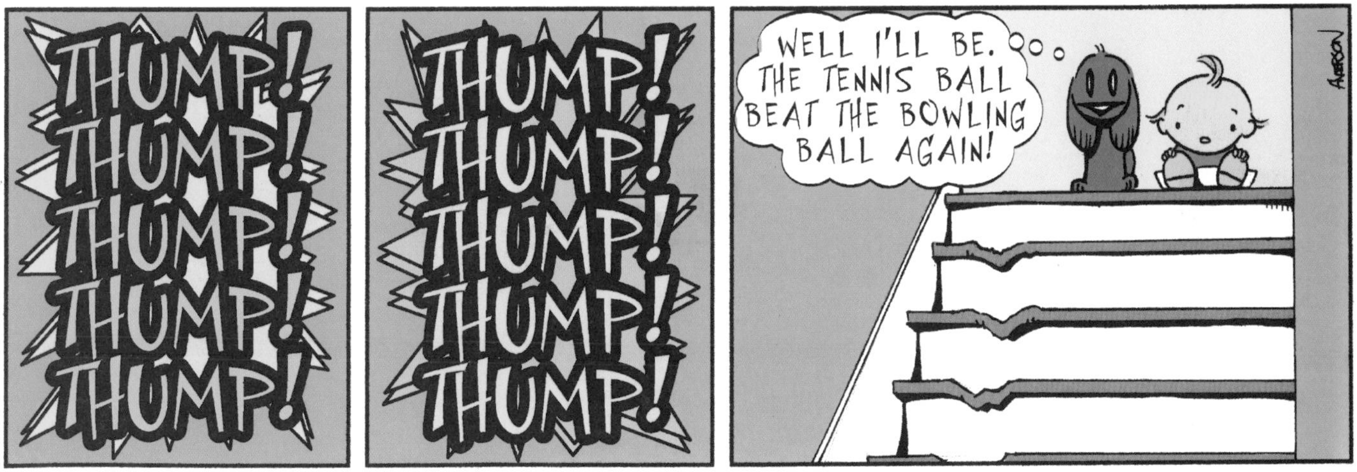
THUMP! THUMP! THUMP! THUMP! THUMP!
THUMP! THUMP! THUMP! THUMP! THUMP!
WELL I'LL BE. THE TENNIS BALL BEAT THE BOWLING BALL AGAIN!

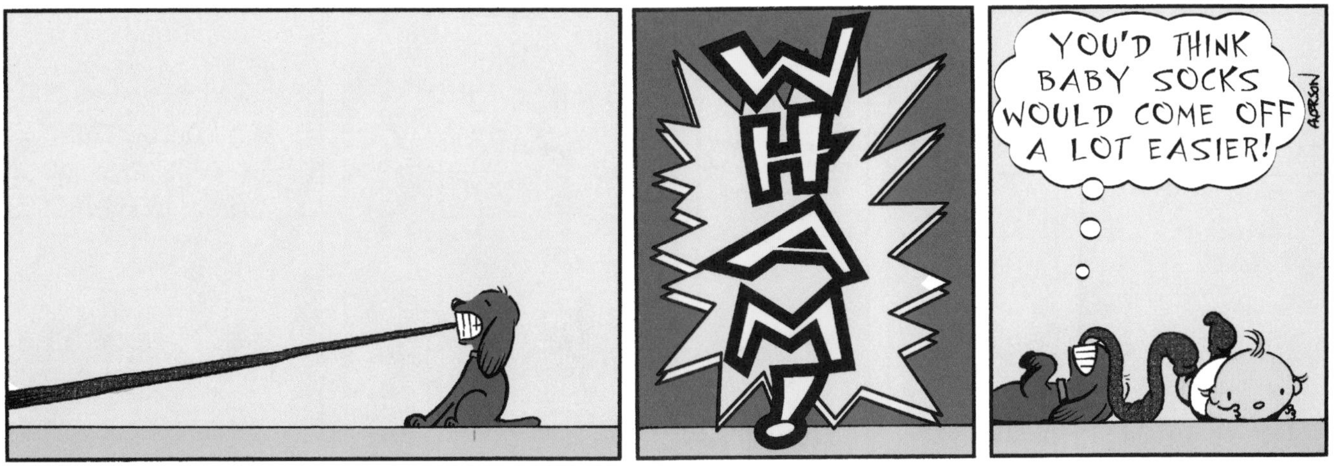
WHAM!
YOU'D THINK BABY SOCKS WOULD COME OFF A LOT EASIER!

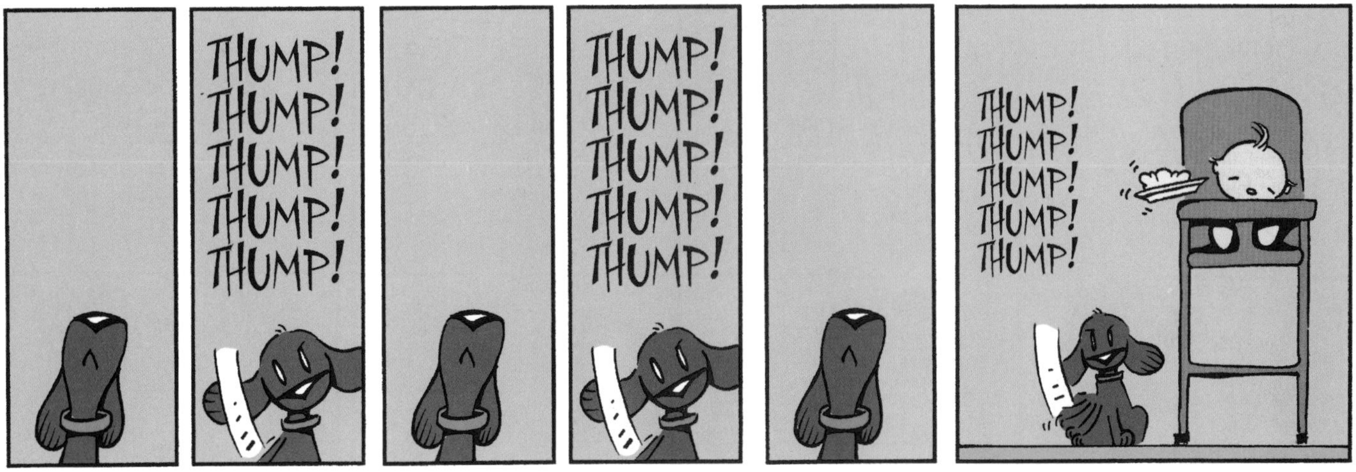
THUMP! THUMP! THUMP! THUMP! THUMP!
THUMP! THUMP! THUMP! THUMP! THUMP!
THUMP! THUMP! THUMP! THUMP! THUMP!

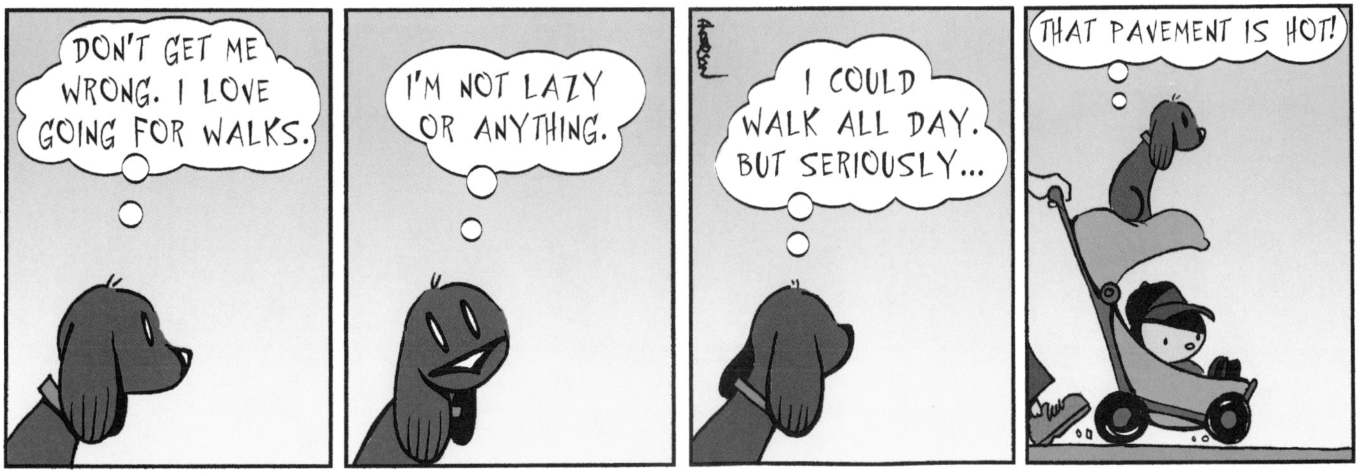
DON'T GET ME WRONG. I LOVE GOING FOR WALKS.
I'M NOT LAZY OR ANYTHING.
I COULD WALK ALL DAY. BUT SERIOUSLY...
THAT PAVEMENT IS HOT!

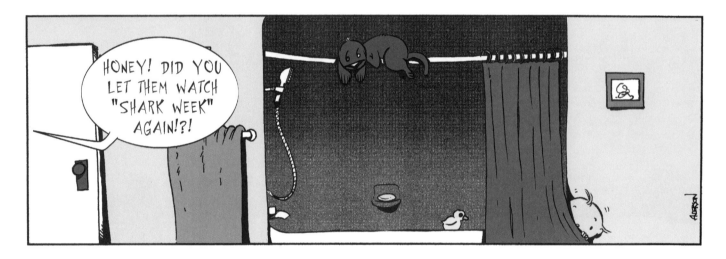

LICK LICK LICK LICK LICK LICK LICK LICK LICK
LICK LICK LICK LICK LICK LICK LICK LICK LICK
LICK LICK LICK LICK LICK LICK LICK LICK LICK
OOOOH! A TELYTUBBY!
SLURP!
NOPE. IT'S JUST DAD.

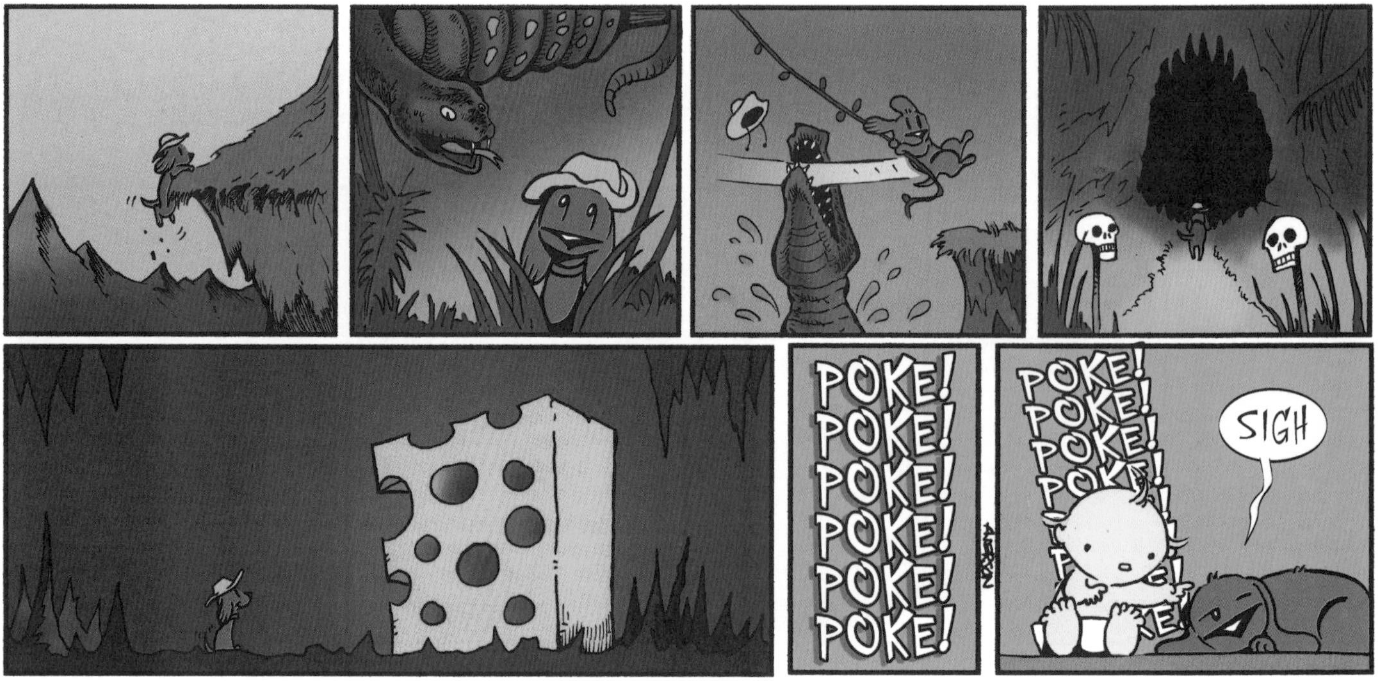
POKE!
POKE!
POKE!
POKE!
POKE!
POKE!
SIGH

106

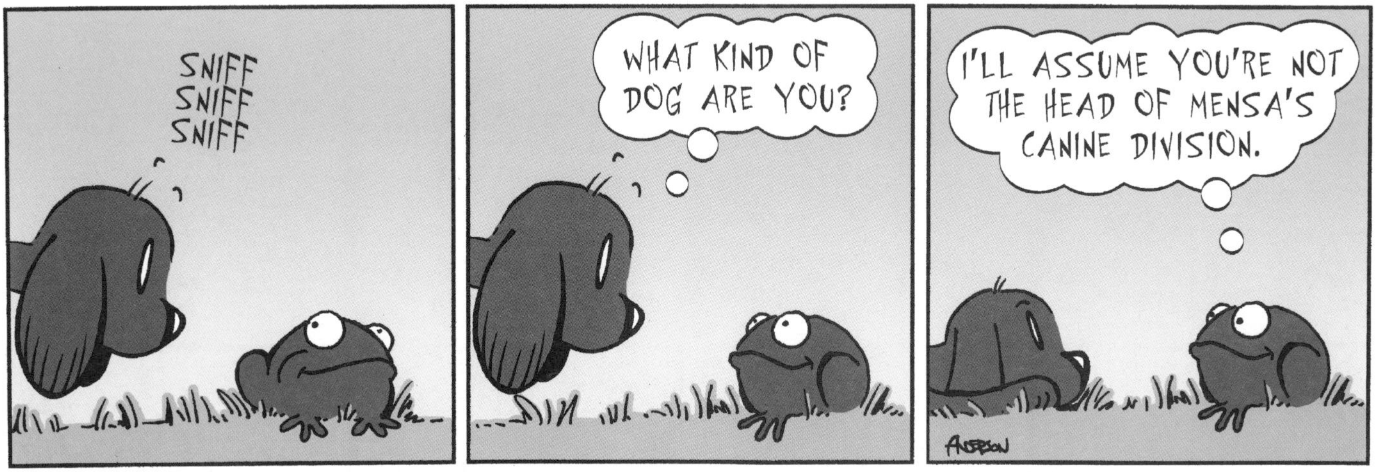
SNIFF
SNIFF
SNIFF
WHAT KIND OF DOG ARE YOU?
I'LL ASSUME YOU'RE NOT THE HEAD OF MENSA'S CANINE DIVISION.

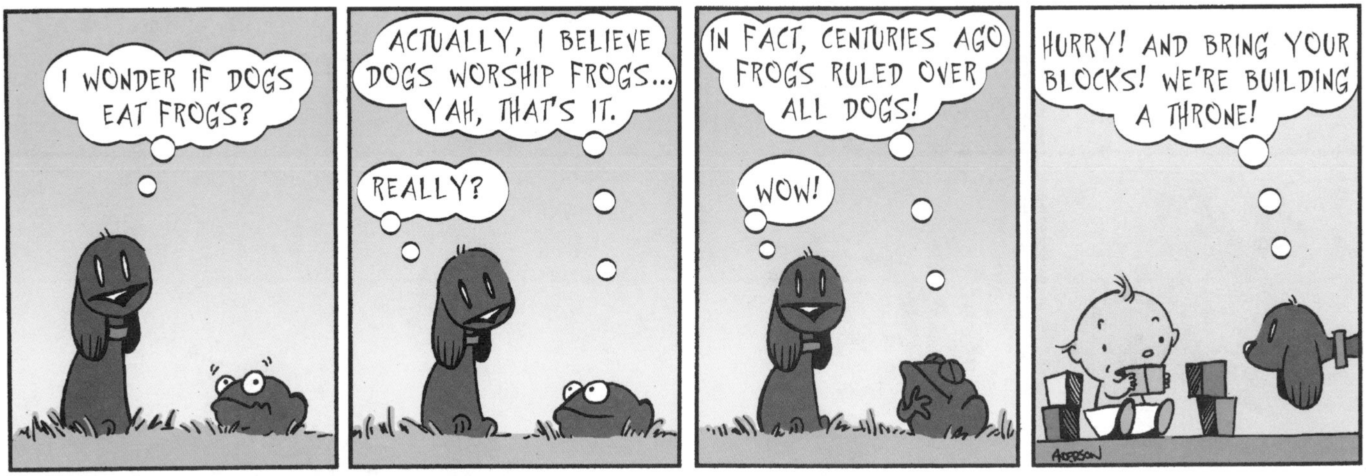
I WONDER IF DOGS EAT FROGS?
ACTUALLY, I BELIEVE DOGS WORSHIP FROGS... YAH, THAT'S IT.
REALLY?
IN FACT, CENTURIES AGO FROGS RULED OVER ALL DOGS!
WOW!
HURRY! AND BRING YOUR BLOCKS! WE'RE BUILDING A THRONE!

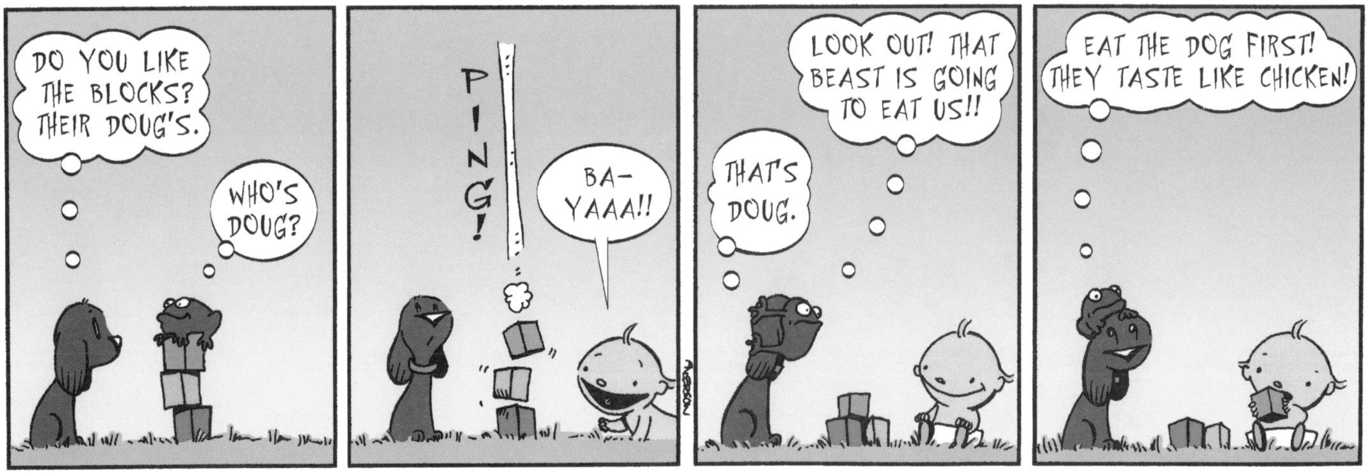
DO YOU LIKE THE BLOCKS? THEIR DOUG'S.
WHO'S DOUG?
PING!
BA-YAAA!!
LOOK OUT! THAT BEAST IS GOING TO EAT US!!
THAT'S DOUG.
EAT THE DOG FIRST! THEY TASTE LIKE CHICKEN!

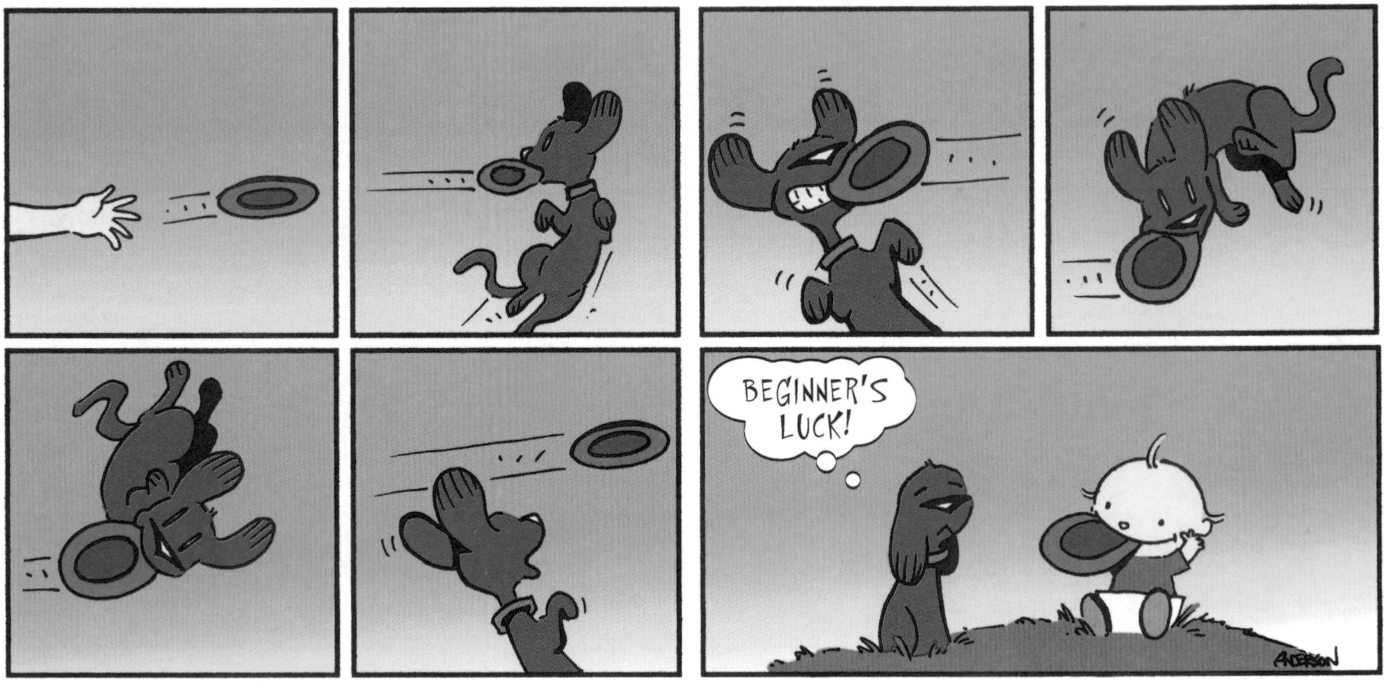
BEGINNER'S LUCK!
ANDERSON

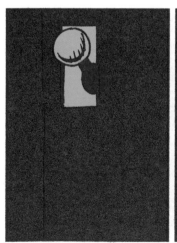

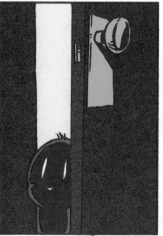

110

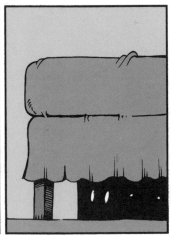

114

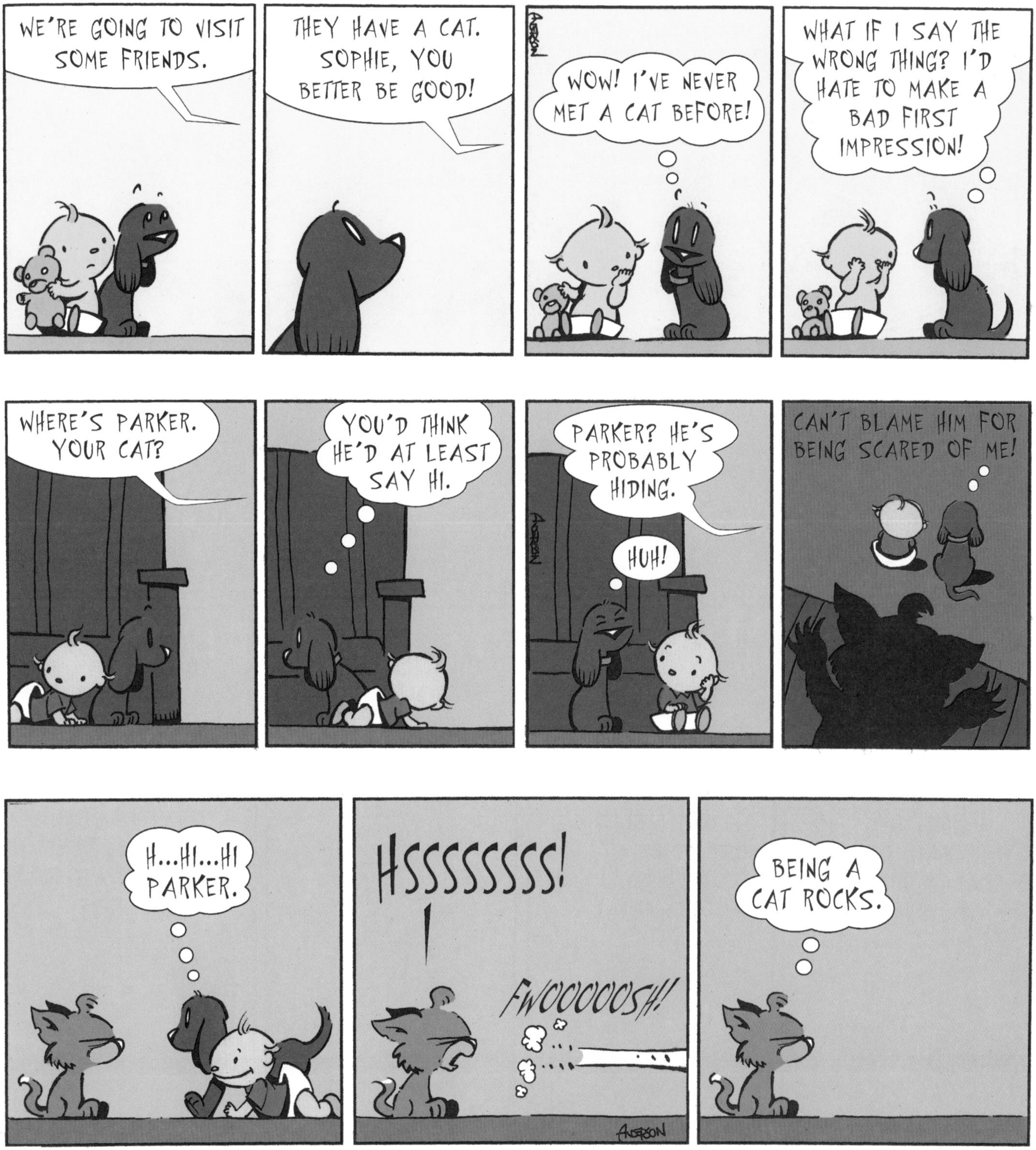
WE'RE GOING TO VISIT SOME FRIENDS.
THEY HAVE A CAT. SOPHIE, YOU BETTER BE GOOD!
WOW! I'VE NEVER MET A CAT BEFORE!
WHAT IF I SAY THE WRONG THING? I'D HATE TO MAKE A BAD FIRST IMPRESSION!
WHERE'S PARKER. YOUR CAT?
YOU'D THINK HE'D AT LEAST SAY HI.
PARKER? HE'S PROBABLY HIDING.
HUH!
CAN'T BLAME HIM FOR BEING SCARED OF ME!
H...HI...HI PARKER.
HSSSSSSSS!
FWOOOOOOSH!
BEING A CAT ROCKS.

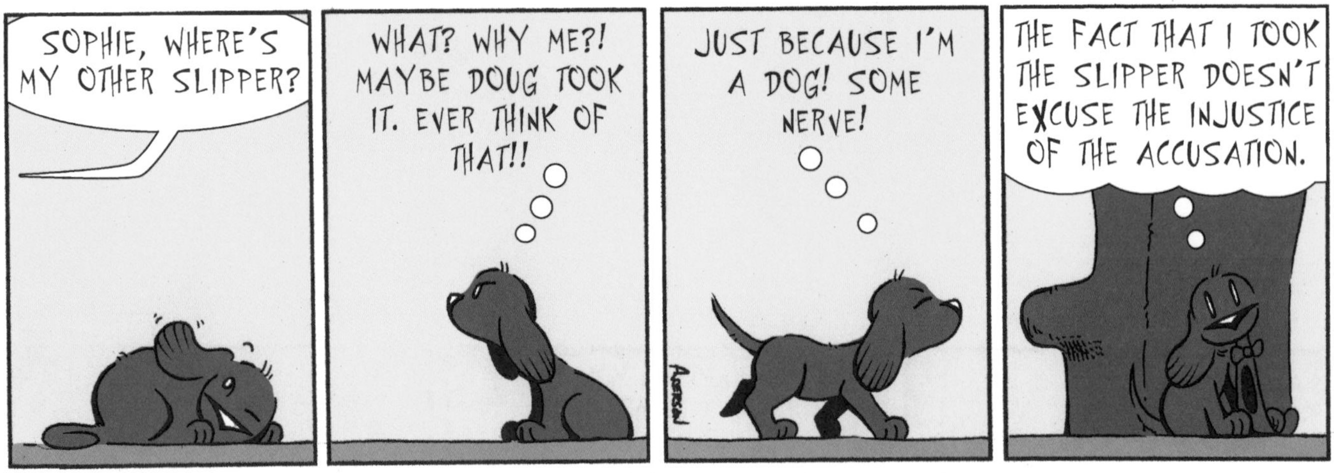
SOPHIE, WHERE'S MY OTHER SLIPPER?
WHAT? WHY ME?! MAYBE DOUG TOOK IT. EVER THINK OF THAT!!
JUST BECAUSE I'M A DOG! SOME NERVE!
THE FACT THAT I TOOK THE SLIPPER DOESN'T EXCUSE THE INJUSTICE OF THE ACCUSATION.

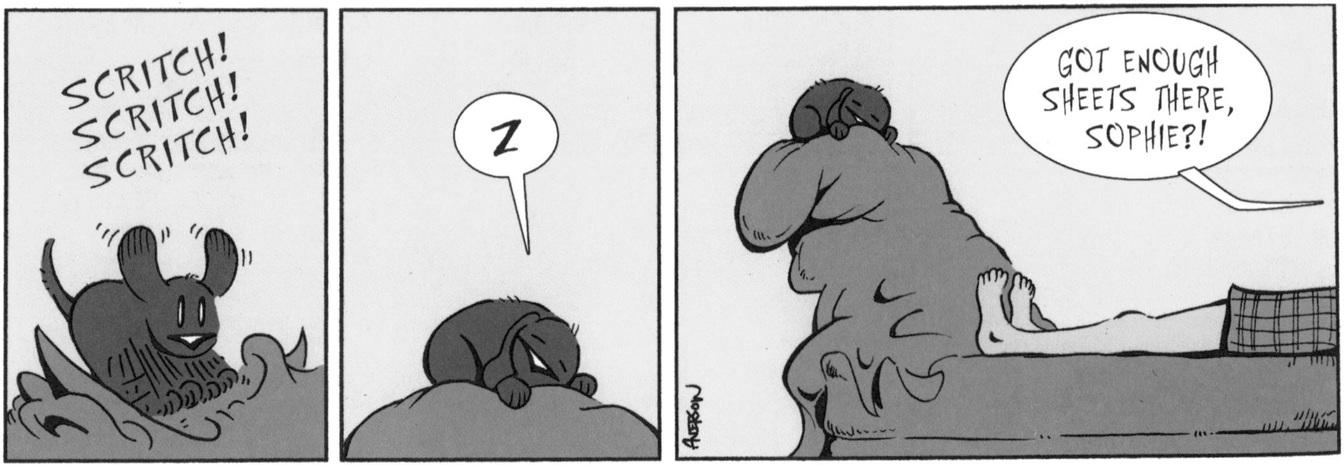
SCRITCH! SCRITCH! SCRITCH!
Z
GOT ENOUGH SHEETS THERE, SOPHIE?!

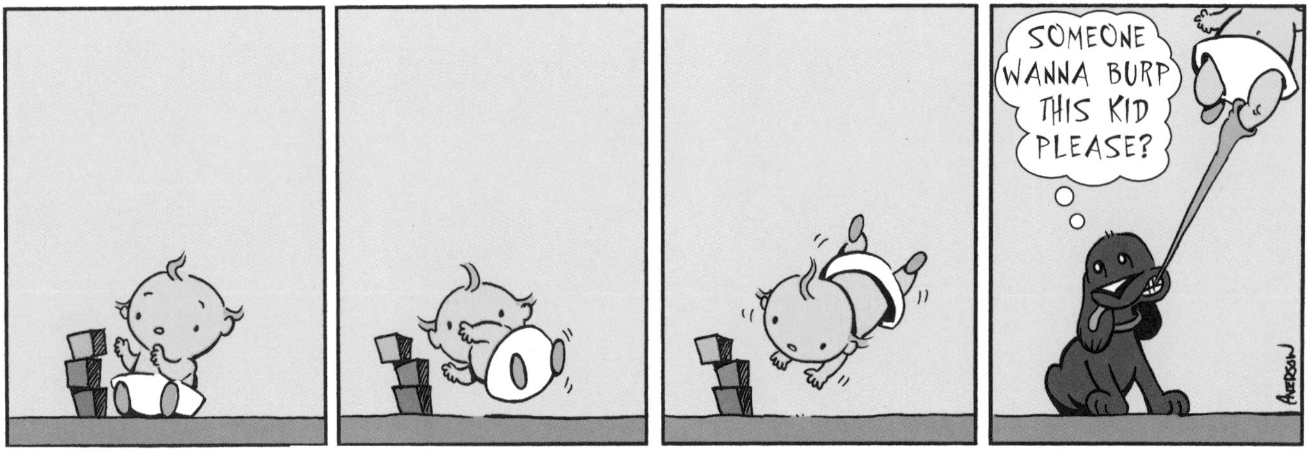
SOMEONE WANNA BURP THIS KID PLEASE?

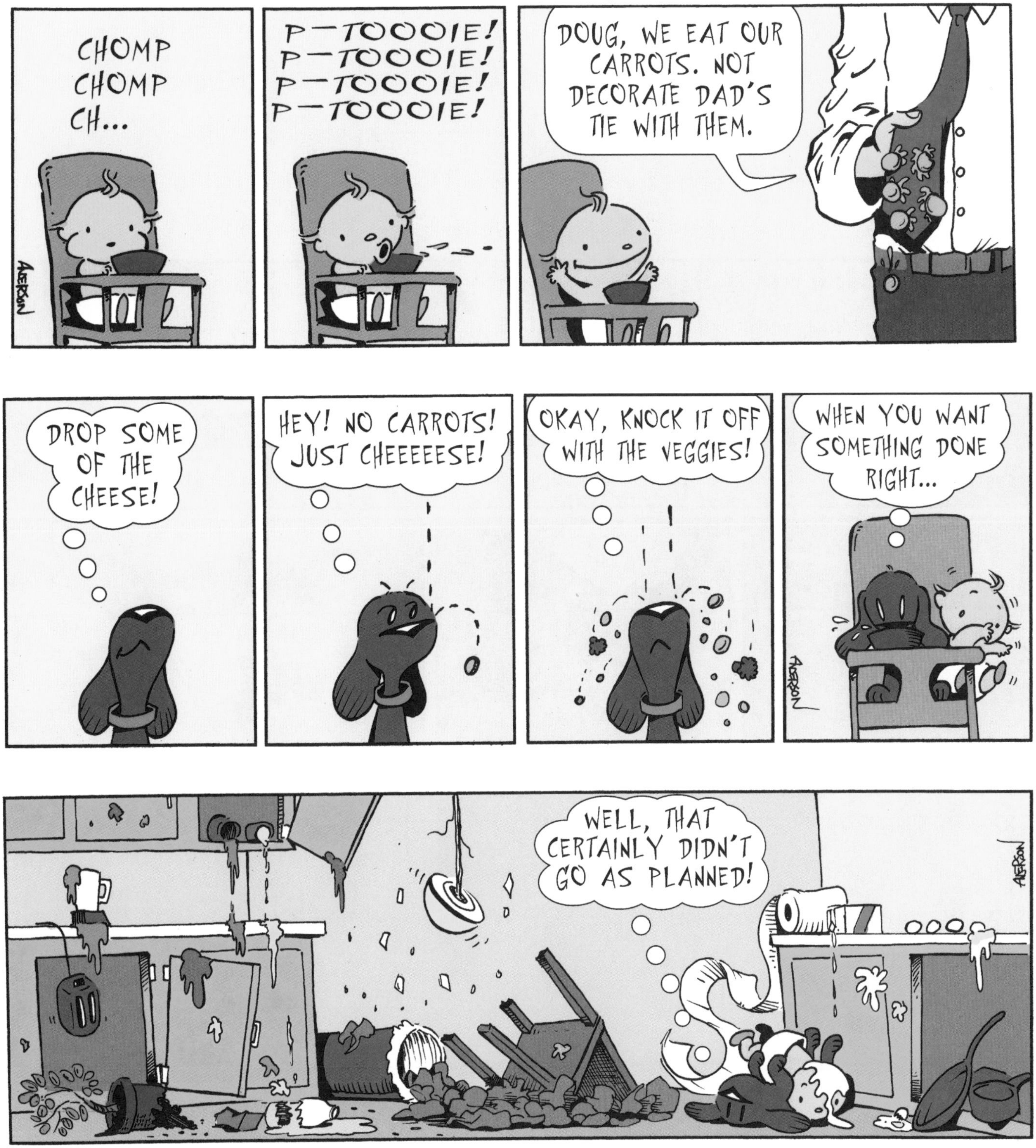
CHOMP
CHOMP
CH...
P—TOOOIE!
P—TOOOIE!
P—TOOOIE!
P—TOOOIE!
DOUG, WE EAT OUR CARROTS. NOT DECORATE DAD'S TIE WITH THEM.
DROP SOME OF THE CHEESE!
HEY! NO CARROTS! JUST CHEEEEESE!
OKAY, KNOCK IT OFF WITH THE VEGGIES!
WHEN YOU WANT SOMETHING DONE RIGHT...
WELL, THAT CERTAINLY DIDN'T GO AS PLANNED!